ARCHITECT OF BEING

EASILY CREATE **YOUR** DREAM LIFE FROM THE FOUNDATION UP

By
JAY BILLIG

Foreword by
BOB PROCTOR

Published by Hasmark Publishing
http://www.hasmarkpublishing.com

Copyright© 2016 by Jay Billig
First Edition, 2016

No part of this book may be reproduced or transmitted in any form or by any means, electronic or mechanical, including photocopying, recording or by any information storage and retrieval system, without written permission from the author, except for the inclusion of brief quotations in a review.

Disclaimer

This book is designed to provide entertainment to readers and is sold purely for entertainment purposes. This is a work of fiction. Characters, names, places, events, incidents and circumstances are a product of the author's imagination and are used fictitiously. Any resemblance to actual persons, living or dead, business establishments, companies or locales is entirely coincidental and is not intended by the author.

The publisher does not have control over and does not assume responsibility for the author or third party websites. Neither the publisher nor the individual author(s) shall be liable for any physical, psychological, emotional, financial, or commercial damages, including, but not limited to special, incidental, consequential, or other damages.

Permission should be addressed in writing to Jay Billig at jay@jaybillig.com

Editor: Justin Spizman
www.justinspizman.com

Cover Design: Jay Billig
www.jaybillig.com

Layout : Anne Karklins
info@annehk.ca

ISBN-13: 978-1-988071-27-5
ISBN-10: 1988071275

To Leroy and Laura
the other half of our family life, co-parents extraordinaire,
without whom we would not know the gift of children.

Contents

Foreword	i
Acknowledgements	iii
Introduction	iv
Preface: Dreaming In Pictures	vii
Part I: Preparing for the Move: Understanding Your Real Self	**1**
Chapter 1: An Ideal Vision	2
Chapter 2: Paradigms, Paradigms, Paradigms	10
Chapter 3: Seeing Your Mind	16
Chapter 4: Intellectual Prowess	22
Chapter 5: Personal Renderings – Illuminated	31
Part II: Laws to Live: The Unbreakable Rules of the Game	**35**
Chapter 6: Law of Oneness	38
Chapter 7: Law of Vibration	40
Chapter 8: Law of Action	42
Chapter 9: Law of Correspondence	44
Chapter 10: Law of Cause and Effect	46
Chapter 11: Law of Compensation	48
Chapter 12: Law of Attraction	50
Chapter 13: Law of Perpetual Transmutation	52
Chapter 14: Law of Relativity	55
Chapter 15: Law of Polarity	58
Chapter 16: Law of Rhythm	60
Chapter 17: Law of Gender	62
Part III: Going With the Flow: Architecture in Action	**64**
Chapter 18: Outside Inside Out	65
Chapter 19: Believing Is Seeing	69
Chapter 20: Choosing Well-Being	75
Chapter 21: Growing Through Fear	79
Chapter 22: Giving Is Receiving	84
Chapter 23: Everyday Ease	90
Chapter 24: Making Music with Life	96

Foreword

Did you know that, by your nature, you are totally set up for success? That you are created with infinite potential – more potential than you could possibly use in your lifetime? Not just you, but every person in the world. In every direction and in every moment, there are opportunities for abundance in every area of your life. Health, happiness and wealth waiting to be chosen by each of us in order to fulfill on our potential and create anything we desire.

I have been in the personal development business for close to half a century. Most of my adult life has been spent studying the mind; why we do the things we do and why we don't do many of the things we know we should do. Although most people, when asked, would tell you they want more health, happiness and wealth in their lives, very few people are aware that they can choose these things and take little or no action on it.

When I met Jay Billig, he communicated his passion for transforming the world and his big dream of sharing what he had been studying for over 25 years with as many people as possible. The train of possibility passed by and, without hesitation, he jumped on board. He had no doubt he was on the right track.

This book is the physical manifestation of Jay's dream and it's a life-changer.

With so much potential locked up inside and unrealized, most people have been living in a squalid rooming house, unaware that it is their birthright to occupy both a mental and physical dream home. Becoming the architect of your own being is the one way to do something about it.

Jay Billig provides every reader with an opportunity to understand themselves and their presence in a perfect and orderly Universe. This book is a practical guide of real how-to's for abundance. Delivered with passion and purpose such that every reader can get something out of it, the wisdom within these pages will help you discover your true potential and be empowered to act on it. I know this book will inspire people worldwide to take positive action in their lives and change the world in so many ways.

Take in all that you can of the ideas and insight you find within these pages and, as Jay points out in the succeeding chapters, take action in order to achieve your goals and live your dreams. Earl Nightingale said, "All you need is the plan, the road map, and the courage to press on to your destination."

This is your road map. Pay attention to and act on the ideas offered. You're about to totally fall in love with your life. Enjoy the journey.

Bob Proctor, best-selling author of *You Were Born Rich*

Acknowledgments

This passion coming from within, outwardly expressed as this book would not have been possible without countless individuals who have been my co-creators on the journey. I am so grateful for each and every one of them and for their contributions to my growth and unfolding. I have been challenged and inspired, moved and expanded, called-out and raised up. If I mentioned each person who has touched me in some way and added to the depth of what is on these pages, it would be longer than the book itself.

I have been supported, encouraged and nurtured every step of the way by my partner Chris, and our deep connection has grown deeper still through the process of realizing this big dream. My sons, Gabriel and Andrew, are my constant reminder to stand up and have my voice heard, to do my best work and be the best possible example I can be for them to follow. They, along with my bonus family, Tressa, Eliora and Ridge, keep me showing up with laughter, a big grin on my face, and a belief that anything is possible.

Introduction

As an architectural designer for over 20 years, I start every interview with a new potential client by asking one singular question: What do you want? While this question seems so simple, the answer can be enormously complicated. But I have found that if we can answer that question, we can then turn words into visuals, thoughts into action, and dreams into reality. Like architecting a house, it feels appropriate to begin this book by asking you the same question about your life: What do you want?

In this book, and in life, you will be guided by an insatiable curiosity and a willingness to explore the unknown. You will have the opportunity to learn things about your world (and yourself) that might seem miraculous, and you might even shift your personal paradigm to see yourself in ways you never considered possible. Throughout this book, I will introduce you to the rules of the game, so to speak, that have been there all along and that are available for each of us to understand. Rounding out the trip will be a whole new – and truly awesome – world of possibilities that open up through understanding and ongoing exploration.

As a child and into early adulthood, one of my favorite pastimes was to draw house plans and dream about what it would be like to live in that space. I spent a considerable amount of time trying to convince my parents that we did not need the attic above our dining room, and that instead it would be way cooler if the ceiling was vaulted to let in more space and light. They did not go for it, but the seeds were planted. While pursuing liturgical music studies in college, I grew very close to a couple who, with the help of a fellow from The Taliesin School of Architecture, undertook a total transformational renovation project, turning a dilapidated rooming house into a prairie-style estate. I got my hands dirty during that process and along the way fell in love with form-following-function design. For me, it was a spiritual experience and I was hooked.

In every place I have ever lived – from my dorm room to homes of a few thousand square feet – I have seen living spaces ready to be awakened by creativity. In 1994, I opened my own business and built everything from furniture and fences to arbors and additions, always looking for ways to add small touches that made a big difference in how to experience the space. I then became a homeowner and immediately proceeded to transform my home into one I was proud to associate with my name. I caught the attention of others and began to receive commissions for larger projects. My hand-drawn plans were no longer adequate, so I went to a couple of friends in architecture and learned the ins and outs of drafting software so I could offer the best service possible. I now call this little idea a career, and have loved every minute of it for the past 20 years.

A curiosity and commitment to learning has remained alongside me every step of the way. I have studied spirituality and spiritual practice in one form or another from the time I was a teenager. When my formal education ended, I turned to books and lectures and have been an active student of both scientific and personal growth teachers since about 1989, taking part in workshops, seminars, and intensive trainings. It was in the late 1990s that I first had the thought of writing a book about the intersection of science and spirituality. This volume is that fulfillment.

This book is like HGTV for your life. When working with clients, the design process begins with identifying what people want and gaining an understanding of how they live their lives so that transformed space can serve their needs.

Recognizing the setting and environment is crucial to making sure you know where you're starting. You then have to lay the right foundation to support that stance. Once the design is complete and you're ready to begin building, the process involves clearing out what is not working and setting new footings to build upon. Everyone is dealing with the same basic materials formulated in an infinite number of ways. Putting it all together involves coordinating the action steps needed to see it through, and the final result is the beautiful manifestation of what began as a dream sometimes weeks, months, or years beforehand. Like envisioning and building a home, creating a dream life is not much different. The same principles are in play, and can be readily applied.

In these pages, you will discover your inner architect, and your ability to design and create anything in your life that you can see in your mind. I feel truly honored that you are taking the time to absorb this material, and thank you for allowing me to hold your hand for a bit as your companion of self discovery. So…what do you want?

To you!

Jay Billig

Preface: Dreaming in Pictures

"A step in the wrong direction is better than staying "on the spot" all your life. Once you're moving forward you can correct your course as you go. Your automatic guidance system cannot guide you when you're stalled, standing still."

~ Maxwell Maltz, MD, FICS

Nothing happens until somebody moves. That somebody is you, and every action you take can be a step toward your goal. Your big goals and dreams are not going to manifest unless, and until, you take action. They can be small baby steps or giant leaps, but rest assured the steps must be taken. The reason why actions speak louder than words is because action is where the rubber meets the road, or where the hammer meets the nail.

Throughout this book, you will read many different references to what makes up all of life. Whether your personal reference point is scientific, theological, spiritual, or some combination of all three, they are all referring to the same thing. For the majority of people, a reference to God or Spirit is familiar, even comforting. Yet for others, even this one reference here will tempt them to put the book down. Some of the other terms used synonymously herein include: Source, Source Energy, Soul, Energy, Universe, Universal Mind, All That Is, The All of Everything, Pure Spirit, Subconscious Mind, Infinite Energy, Infinite Mind, Infinite Intelligence, Divine Oneness, and Love. Many others exist, so you can use whatever terms suit your understanding of our One Source, and pick up a few new ones for a broader view! There is no judgment at all for where you are on this spectrum – you are welcome to dive in and discover not only where you are, but also where you never imagined you would find yourself.

Source Energy is in motion all around, with, to, and through you. It is with the thoughts in your conscious mind that you make it into positive or negative power. Everything, in its wholeness, has both positive and negative, but only one of those polarities can be expressed in any given moment. Your thoughts, then, are what determine whether you experience things as positive or negative. The choice is up to you.

We are constantly being bombarded with information and ideas from every source imaginable that flows our way. Even if negativity surrounds you, you don't have to let it in. Don't even give it a second thought; instead, focus on the positive aspects of your experience. If you internalize positive ideas and reject negative ones, you will be far better off than most people.

Your senses and mental toolbox reside in your conscious mind. You're connected to the rest of the world through your senses and this is where you do your thinking. It is here that you can decide what you want to focus on. Your thinking mind has the ability to ignore or absorb. Claim the positive and take it all in.

The thoughts you choose to impress on the subconscious mind must be taken in. The subconscious cannot ignore anything, and it treats everything that comes its way the same, with complete acceptance. Whether you imagine it or observe it, the subconscious mind takes it in and assumes it is real. The subconscious mind only has one response to whatever information you give it, and that is an unequivocal YES!

It is your repetitive thoughts and ideas that, when impressed on the subconscious mind, control your vibration. The vibration of your body – feelings – comes directly from the subconscious mind as a result of what was absorbed. Negative ideas will produce a negative vibration, and likewise positive ideas will have you feeling really good. Which one would you prefer?

Vibration and attraction cannot be separated. Whatever vibration your mind and body is in will determine exactly what you put out, and thus exactly what you attract. If you are in a negative vibration it is not possible to attract positive energy. You must move into a positive vibration, which you do by changing the ideas you choose to continually focus on. There is not a single person or thing that can force you to think anything you do not want to think. Free will is yours, so you can think anything you want.

It is the mind that controls the body – all the time. The body is like a toy, a puppet that is literally hypnotized by the mind. However, by understanding how the mind works, you put yourself in the driver's seat. You can create the world around you rather than being a slave to it.

The alignment of positive thoughts in your conscious mind with the positive vibration in your subconscious mind creates actions that are also positive. In turn, your total positive alignment must produce positive results. What you send out is what you get back. This is what we will focus on in this book. You will learn how to control your thoughts, thereby creating your reality – the life of your dreams.

This is a life-long journey you're on. Every step of the way is an opportunity to find a better way to do whatever it is you are doing. Choose the next best version of yourself and take action to create lasting results.

Part I

PREPARING FOR THE MOVE: UNDERSTANDING YOUR REAL SELF

"All the answers you seek lie within."
~ Mike Dooley

Most likely in more than a few conversations in your lifetime, you have been asked the question, "Who are you?" And if you are like most people, in an automatic response, you rattle off your name. You are so much more than your name, and even so much more than your body and soul.

In this section you will open the doors to seeing who you actually are and exploring what makes you tick. You will turn on the lights to your biggest dreams and discover what keeps you on track, and what keeps you from moving forward. Your ability to see and understand the inner workings of your mind will all be revealed to you, as well as the tools you've had at your disposal your entire life and probably didn't even know about. You will get to see yourself as you have never seen yourself before, and create whatever "you" your heart desires.

Chapter 1

AN IDEAL VISION

"Creation begins with imagination."
~ Scott Noelle

What do you really want?

How many times have you asked yourself that question and come up with an answer? For most people, this is not a question to even entertain, much less an answer they have given any serious consideration.

Believing in what's possible rather than in what you are observing is the first place to start. What beliefs do you hold about the world? What are the reasons you believe as you do? Your beliefs are ready to step in and hold you back from setting goals, stopping you in your tracks before you even begin. Like all energy, which is in a constant state of change, so are our beliefs. They can and must be changed to serve you as you move forward in this new direction.

You are connected to an infinite source of supply. You can create anything in physical form that you can dream of in your mind. In fact, the creative process begins when you first have the thought, summoning Source into action to fulfill on it for you.

At birth, children are programmed to dream, to fantasize about what their world might become. Their natural inclination is for fantasy, and when they dream, they are convinced their dreams will become reality. They have not yet been influenced by the outside world, by people who tell them to stop dreaming and get with the program. That is, until they are subjected to the views of the adults they look to for guidance. Before long, they are told to stop dreaming and focus on school. And when their fantasy world is suppressed, it becomes less and less available for their daily use. Did this ever happen to you?

The problem with teaching kids to stop fantasizing is that fantasy is the first step to freedom. So, suppressing this practice inadvertently limits freedom and perpetuates a lie that has been passed down from one generation to the next. A vast majority of adults had their fantasy world cut short as school-aged children, and so they never learned to trust their inherent goodness and connection to their Source. Now is the time to re-engage your fantastic abilities and start to dream.

Keep asking yourself the question: What do I really want? And keep in mind your Infinite Source does not care how big or how small your desires are. It will do its part to give you exactly what you are asking for. Dig in deep. You can take yourself way back to when you were a child. What did you dream about being when you "grew up" that perhaps got thwarted? What's on your bucket list that you're still waiting to do "some day"? How about all of the things you've come up with that will make the world a better place? What about the genius ideas you've jotted down on a napkin along the way? Have you recorded the album you've been thinking about? What about the book you've always wanted to write? Do you live in your dream home? Where and when do you go on vacation? How do you get there?

It is very important to ask that question from the place of the thing you want rather than from the position you are in. From where you are, your view is very limited, but when looked at from your fantasy, you can tap into the Infinite and bring forth your burning desires. It is from this place that your vision of the future will help you find your way to your dreams.

Leveling the Playing Field

When setting goals or creating visions of your dream life, there are different levels of goals that you can set:

1. *Level one* goals are things that you already know how to do or have.
2. *Level two* goals are things that you think you can do, and that follow in logical order from where you are.
3. *Level three* goals are from your fantasies, big goals that energize and scare you at the same time. A level three goal is what you want to focus on and what will both inspire you and cause big growth.

Let's say you want to buy a new home. You have your eye set on a new townhouse in the central part of your city. You currently own a townhouse about a mile away that you have had for about five years, since it was built. The townhouse you want to buy is new construction and you really like living in a newly built place. You set a goal to sell your current home and buy the new place in the next 3 months. The new place is really great and your current place is very desirable for someone who wants to buy a gently used home. The goal you have set is a level one goal because you already know how to do it, and there is no growth involved. You have already experienced a new townhouse and have lived in it for five years. This is not to say you should not get the new home, just that it does not constitute an ideal vision type goal.

Consider another example. You have been working at the same job as a computer programmer for about three years and you have decided it is time for a change. You have updated your resume and set a goal of getting a job earning about 20% more at a different company. In your field, this is not unheard of, in fact it is expected that you move up the ranks from business to business. While on first look a 20% jump in compensation seems large, it is actually the next logical step for you and would constitute a level two goal.

It seems like a stretch, but it is not very inspiring. You will probably get bored there and long for something much bigger within another three years.

Being that a level three goal is enormously powerful, how do you know what constitutes this type of goal? To start, it must fulfill your burning desire. It is only with that level of desire that there is any hope for following through and actually achieving it. It is also something you have never done before, a place you have never been. It will be scary, exciting, and heart pumping. The truth is that if you know how to do it, it is not a worthy goal.

Planting the Seeds of Thought

The creative process begins with an idea, a thought in the imagination. Everything that now exists was first a thought, a fantasy, outside the realm of what you already know to exist. As the fantasy is entertained, dreamed about, written down, and repeated over and over, you ask the question, "Am I able to accomplish this?" Considering that you are a manifestation of Infinite Energy with infinite potential, there is really no question of whether or not you are able. But you've got to be willing to do whatever it takes to manifest your fantasy in physical form. With belief, your fantasy turns into a goal, and through repetition you get emotionally involved. You turn it over to the subconscious mind and the perpetual transmutation of energy goes to work, causing your idea energy to become physical energy. When you believe it, your actions change and your goal becomes a fact, completing the creative cycle.

Here is the creative cycle at a glance:
- Idea – fantasy – in the imagination
- Keep dreaming about it, write it down
- Ask yourself, "Am I willing?"
- Belief turns fantasy into a goal
- Repetition has you fall in love with it

- Subconscious mind takes over
- Actions change and it becomes a fact

Every step of the way, outside influences will try to steer you off course. You've got to close yourself off to them and refuse to let any external circumstances or conditions have any say. Let nothing stop you, and let your own desire be your guide.

As you are considering your big goal, set aside consideration for how much it will cost or where the money will come from. Give no consideration whatsoever as to how you are going to do it, but instead focus on what stirs your heart. Passion should lead the way. You are setting in motion a command to the Universe and by law, if you keep the picture of it in your mind and step in its direction, it must be brought into physical form.

There are a number of very effective ways to set goals, and for every one of them the key is to be extremely specific. Source responds to definite desires, backed by belief and action. If you have a goal for any manner of abundance in your life, think about exactly what it is that you desire to have or to be. Always frame it in positive words and positive outcomes. Tap into the feeling of what it is like to already have it and believe it is inevitable.

Choose your words carefully. For example, using verbs in their active (gerund, -ing) form will have you experiencing whatever it is more easily since they are all about movement. "I am" and "I have" are some of the most powerful words available to us. Saying, "I want" will give you the experience of wanting, not the experience of having or being. Also, skip how you will do it all together, as this is will only distract you from your goal. Mike Dooley coined the term, "the cursed hows," for exactly this reason. Simply rest assured you are ready to jump right in and are able to achieve your goal.

As an example, if you have a goal of earning more money and eliminating debt, determine exactly how much you desire to have.

More money can come to you as a nickel in the street or as earning $1,000,000 per month for the phenomenal service you provide. Even the mention of debt will have you experiencing debt. A very effective way to think about it is to determine how much you desire to pay off and, beyond any income goals, talk about attracting an *extra* X dollars into your life.

Write a list of all your wants and desires for each area of your life (work, home, community). Go over it and from that big list, narrow it down to the one that you really want – the one that totally stirs your heart and soul. It is also important to make sure that the desires from different areas of your life are in harmony with each other.

After you have identified your number one goal, write it out in present tense in the following format: I am so happy and grateful now that… (my big dream is manifested in physical form). Create a card to carry around with you all the time – a goal card. On it, write out your goal clearly and concisely so that a stranger reading it will get the same mental picture you have in your mind. Not sure how to make a goal card? You can go to jaybillig.com right now and download your very own goal card for free!

Here are some examples of powerful goal statements that you can use for inspiration when creating your own:

- I am so happy and grateful now that I have a continual supply of effective leads and an exponentially increasing list of well-served clients who recommend me to their colleagues and friends. I'm having fun and effortlessly earning $10,000 or more per week.
- I am so happy and grateful now that I am in leadership for a non-profit organization whose mission is to educate women and girls worldwide, empowering them to be leaders and change-makers in their communities.
- I am so happy and grateful now that I am sharing my life with a partner I love deeply and adore, and who deeply loves and adores me.

- I am so happy and grateful now that I have harmonious, mutually respectful, and loving interactions with my children and extended family.
- I am so happy and grateful now that I am an international best-selling author, effectively communicating with millions of people all over the world.
- I am so happy and grateful now that I am easily earning $1,000,000 or more per month, being of exceptional service to humanity, and for the mutual benefit of all involved.
- I am so happy and grateful now that I am part of a team of people harmoniously creating new homes for tens of thousands of people across the continent.
- I am so happy and grateful now that I have my own salon where we are serving hundreds of satisfied clients every month, and where we are booked up for months in advance. I am easily earning in a month what I used to earn in a year, and I am having so much fun doing it!
- I am so happy and grateful now that I have a beautiful home with a separate bedroom for each of our children, a guest room, three or more bathrooms, and a master suite on the main level. I love cooking and eating together in the large, open kitchen and family room, as we spend time celebrating each other's lives all with a canopy of gorgeous shade trees and a hammock for resting and relaxing.

Carry your goal card around with you always and read it several times every day. Share it with people who will support you and your vision for yourself. As a note of caution, there will most likely be people in your life who do not share your dream of transformation, or what you want to create. If you don't get full support, just let it go with them and surround yourself with people who are supportive.

From your list of wants and desires, you can also create a vision board, or dream board. This is a very helpful tool because we think in pictures. For each area of your life, take the top one or two desires and create a visual representation of them on your vision board. Searching online for pictures is easy and fun, and it allows you to imprint images in your mind that you will eventually make your reality. Print out the images you like and put them together on a piece of poster board, which you will place in a location where you see it many times each day.

Similarly, put pictures of what you want as your screen saver for your desktop, laptop, tablet, and phone. Having it as a constant reminder will instill the belief of it into the subconscious mind.

Think about your goal several times every day and picture yourself already having it. This brings you and your vision closer together, into the same vibration. You must really want it, picture it, and think about it, as what you ruminate on most will come into physical form.

You might be one of the few people who already has an ideal vision for your life, and if so, that's great! You can still use some of the tools here to help you up the ante. And if you're not one of those people, there's no time like the present to take a step forward and create goals. Focusing on an ideal vision will help to guide you in the direction of your ultimate goals. You'll begin to see differences in your life that are the results of your newly founded habits and actions. This starts by identifying goals in all areas of your life, and focusing on the one you would most like to manifest. Use your goal card to embed the goal in your subconscious, and think as if the goal has already been met. Only then will you create a shift, and begin the process of manifesting the life of your dreams.

This first chapter has laid the foundation for living your best life. A large part of doing this involves understanding that our thoughts shape our reality. Thoughts occur in our conscious mind, and, when taken in, become embedded in our subconscious mind. Some of these thoughts become habitual, and produce the paradigms that rule our lives. It is important that these paradigms support our goals; for if not, they will stop progress. We will explore how to align these paradigms in the next chapter.

Chapter 2

PARADIGMS, PARADIGMS, PARADIGMS

"When we activate something without resistance, it comes fast."
~ Esther Hicks

A paradigm is a pattern of something, or a typical example or model. For our purposes here, a paradigm is a pattern of habits. These habits are ideas that are so fixed in the subconscious mind we don't even think about doing them. Paradigms are what control our habitual actions. There are many times when we do things we don't want to do, thereby producing results we don't really want, all because of the paradigms that are at work in the background.

As a child, the people surrounding you provided the basic fundamental guidelines for your life. You took it all in because you were wired to do so. The adults who raised you – generations of them – taught you what they knew because they were wired to do so. You were programmed, even before birth in your DNA, by the ways of your ancestors and there was nothing you could do about it. You are now programmed – every cell of your being – with both genetics and conditioning.

There are countless examples of people having all the information they need to make changes to improve their lives, and yet not actually doing anything about it. There are those who start in on a new regimen, only to see it quickly fade. The truth is, it is not really their fault at all, but rather their ignorance about what controls their behavior. The culprit is their operating system, also known as their paradigm. The good news is that when the operating system is updated, it can then unleash a whole new way of effective and efficient existence.

In human beings, paradigms can hold you back, much like if you were driving your car with the parking brake partially engaged. You can go, but it is sluggish at best, and when you disengage the brake, only then can the car quickly accelerate. Paradigms keep people operating in a very inefficient manner, held back from their infinite true potential.

You can probably think of some people who get really amazing results, and yet are not exactly considered to be the brightest bulbs in the bunch. Everyone wants to know their secret, but in truth, it really comes down to their paradigms. They have either consciously (or by default) gotten into alignment with the paradigm that produces exactly what they want. The paradigm drives the bus, so to speak, and they may not even be aware that they are merely a passenger on board.

Shifting Your Paradigms

To skyrocket your results, you must understand paradigms and be able to replace the old, ineffective ones with new, effective ones. So how do you do that? The first step is to understand that all of your habitual behaviors are the results of paradigms. Once you recognize this and are willing to take an objective look at the results in your life, you can work to identify the paradigms that limit you. One at a time (or two, max), begin a new habit that replaces one that is not serving you. Over time, you will begin to attain your desired results.

Keep in mind, though, that paradigms are not simply behaviors. They reside much deeper in your inner being. They are deeply engrained groups of habits about yourself that you might not even be aware you have. Your results tell the truth about your paradigms, and you must be willing to take an honest look and make changes in order to secure different results.

Many people are locked into a particular way of experiencing life that by all accounts would be described as unpleasant at best. Because paradigms are so strong, they can keep you in the comfort of the familiar even if it is, in fact, a very uncomfortable place to be.

Paradigms are very powerful and will talk you right out of the changes you wish to make. When you start to make changes toward a new world, your operating system needs an update, and you've got to be willing to stick it out until your new procedures are firmly in place. Even then, other paradigms may rear their ugly heads and do their best to stick to business as usual. They will do everything to keep you going with the comforts of what you know, simply because it feels familiar. This will not serve you well in the long run, but then again, your paradigms aren't all that concerned with future results.

Transformational change takes persistence and concentrated effort through repetition of new, effective ways of doing what you want to do. Keep your vibration in harmony with your goal and take steps toward it. They may be the same steps over and over again – but repetition is the way to reprogram your operating paradigms.

Paradigms: Conscious or Subconscious?

There is a very important distinction to point out about the mind as it relates to paradigms. Your conscious mind is the part of you that relates to your environment, through your five senses and intellectual faculties. It has the ability to accept or reject anything entering it. However, the subconscious mind, where paradigms reside, accepts everything that is impressed upon it and then automatically expresses those things through the body. It is the vibration of the subconscious mind, or paradigms, that push the body to behave in a particular way and produce very specific, predictable results.

The good news here is that what you purposely impress upon the subconscious mind will also be expressed with and through your body. The subconscious mind makes no distinction between facts and fantasy – it treats them all the same and, with repetition, programs itself and operates accordingly. Even more good news is that you have the power to change your programming and get the results you desire – those that are in perfect alignment with your goals and big dreams.

So, if you want to enjoy better results, you have to change your paradigms. You can change behaviors all day long and may even get some improved results for a while, but unless you change the paradigm, the change will only be temporary. You'll eventually revert back to your old behaviors. Understanding the way the subconscious mind is programmed will allow you to begin to change it and reprogram yourself with new habits and improved paradigms.

The Culture of Paradigms

We refer to our attitudes, habits, beliefs, and expectations as culture, and culture is another layer of existence that creates your paradigms. Because of cultural programming and accepted standards, you are set up for being able to navigate the world around you. You are programmed to be able to see your current realm, how it operates, and how to navigate within it.

Your internal compass is what guides you, and it (not outside conditions) is behind the results you are getting. So, bringing about a paradigm shift is changing to a new operating procedure – a new compass – or an entirely new realm of being. Using a new compass can create a new type of journey. Change your paradigms and you will change the world that you are creating.

Since paradigms control your logical thinking, simply employing the creative power of your imagination is often not enough to manifest change. This is because you are often seeing things from where they are – present results – and not from the viewpoint of what you want to create. This causes people to get into repeating cycles from which they cannot disconnect. The path to freedom takes a willingness to change, the courage to honestly and objectively see what behaviors are not working, and the drive and persistence to build a new paradigm that will replace the old one.

Finding Your Positive Paradigms

Paradigms are not always negative. In fact, you may find many positive paradigms in your life. Just as negative paradigms create negative outcomes, positive paradigms create positive ones. Your paradigms attract circumstances and conditions that serve up more of whatever they need to contribute to their continued existence. Learning to alter your paradigms is the only way to change whatever situation you are in. If you can create positive paradigms, you can invoke more and more positive vibrations into your very existence. They are fun and easy to create, and are self-serving once you do.

This begs the question: which habits do you want to change? If you are being honest with yourself, you will probably come up with a very long list that could use some attention. You've had a lifetime to practice certain paradigms, and it will take some time to establish new ones, so you must have faith and persistence. The best way to address paradigms is generally one at a time. If you try to change too many at once, it is very likely you will not change any of them at all.

Simply eliminating a negative habit will not suffice. In order to bring about permanent change, a negative habit must be replaced with a positive one. If you only remove one, the current paradigm will kick into gear and replace it with another negative one.

A picture in the subconscious mind is what determines your results and informs your perception of what is possible. So continually impressing a new and wonderful picture of what you want onto the subconscious mind is a necessary action to take in order to get a big change in your behavior and your results. It is a picture of your beautiful new self.

Paradigms are part of what it means to be a human being. Understanding that they exist and being able to recognize them in yourself is a huge step to taking control of your life. Choosing to transform yourself by replacing negative paradigms that are not serving you with positive ones is very empowering and can act as your ticket to freedom. You will begin to see yourself in a very different way, and with practice be able to bring about lasting changes in your life with a whole new realm of possibilities.

Now that you understand paradigms and how they shape your reality, it is time to turn our attention to the mind-body connection, and the role it plays in fulfilling our destiny.

Chapter 3

SEEING YOUR MIND

"Whatever your level of understanding, it will not change the fact that you already create the life you lead from the thoughts you think; this truth can't be escaped. By understanding it, however, you acknowledge yourself to be the creator of your experience."
~ Mike Dooley

Picture your home. What does it look like? What color is it? Is it made of wood, brick, stucco, or stone? Now picture your kitchen. What does your stove look like? What color are your cabinets? What is behind the cabinet door to the left of your kitchen sink?

We think in pictures, which is what allows you to see all of these things clearly. Now, what does your mind look like? Try to describe it. Not so easy, is it? Seeing your mind is not exactly like picturing a tangible and real life image.

You might get an image of the brain when you think about the mind. However, the brain is not the mind. Rather, it is the electronic control center of the body. The mind permeates every cell of the body and is a direct link to the Universal Mind or Source Energy. The mind is pure energy and the body (including the brain) is the physical manifestation of the same pure energy. The body does not control the mind, but rather the body is a vehicle of the mind.

This can be confusing to understand because there is no image of the mind to reference. In the mid-1930s, Dr. Thurman Fleet, a chiropractor and founder of Concept Theory and Conceptology, proposed a picture that could represent the mind. This picture should help to shed the confusion of the unknown. Having a model to work with will bring about understanding as we study the mind. His proposed image is referenced below.

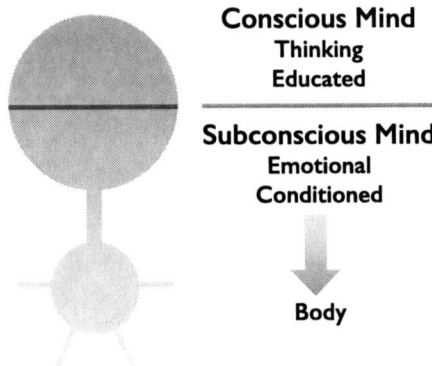

The Top Half

The top half of the larger circle represents the conscious mind, also referred to as the thinking mind or the educated mind. This is where your senses and your intellect are connected. This is the source of your free will and the place where you can originate thoughts. It is where you choose your vibration. The conscious mind has the ability to take in or shut out any idea that comes its way.

There is nothing outside of you – no person, event, or circumstance – that can cause you to think anything you do not want to think. You are the source of your own thoughts and are able to decide what your conscious mind grasps. You then, by use of your conscious mind, are the reason for the results recognized in your life, either by choice or by blind acceptance.

The Bottom Half

The bottom half of the larger circle represents the subconscious mind, also called the emotional mind or conditioned mind. This is your hook up to Infinite Intelligence. It is your power supply and your warp drive all in one. It operates throughout every cell of your body and accepts everything it is given as real. Whatever your conscious mind chooses to take in must be accepted by your subconscious mind.

This is the part of you that operates by law – every time for every person. What is impressed upon the subconscious mind is automatically expressed through you as feelings and actions. This is the realm of paradigms; your automatic, habitual ways of being. They reside in the subconscious mind along with your beliefs, self-image, and feelings. Any thought that is repeatedly delivered to the subconscious mind will become fixed as part of your system software. Any ideas that are fixed in this part of you will continue to express themselves as habits unless, and until, new ones replace them. Once fixed in the subconscious mind, ideas do not need any conscious attention to activate and express through the body.

The subconscious mind is pure Source Energy or Spirit. In actuality, everything is pure energy, including your physical form, forever in motion and transformation. As you know, we think in pictures, and so to have an image of the mind helps to bring about true understanding. Your essence as pure Source Energy is perfect. It contains every potential of All That Is and it is your birthright to discover and manifest it into your wildest dreams.

The Smaller Circle

Finally, the smaller circle represents the body. Observed through the senses, the body may seem like it is the largest part of the image, but it is actually the most limited piece. It is the physical expression of you and your mind. It is a vehicle of the mind, your physical residence. Your consciously (or unconsciously) chosen ideas, thoughts, and images move your body into action. Those actions (or inactions) then determine your results.

To wrap it all together, the whole process of mind-body integration goes like this:

- There is a power flowing into your conscious mind where you can both create new ideas and accept or reject any idea that comes into it from the outside.
- Whatever you impress upon the subconscious, whether fact or fantasy, your subconscious will accept as real.
- As you get emotionally involved with it, your vibration changes and the body, which is a vehicle of the mind, must move into action.
- This action then causes a reaction from Source Energy and produces your results.

The mind image of the stickperson is a very powerful tool. Study it and commit it to memory so that every time you think of yourself, you see it on the screen of your mind. And then, as you observe other people, see the image as well. Being able to see the mind will help you to understand it and eventually change it in order to recognize better outcomes.

While behavior is the outward expression that leads to results, it is really secondary to paradigms, which are the primary cause of those results. Changing behaviors may offer some temporary changes in results, but because paradigms are so deeply engrained in a person, they are what must be changed to effect permanent improvement.

For most people, the outside received through the senses is their guide; how they gauge their whole existence. This is very unfortunate because the senses only offer a small glimpse of what is possible. This paradigm locks people into a place where they think the external world is all there is. If you observe other people, objectively looking at their behavior and results, you will be able to understand what is going on in their subconscious mind. To help people change what they are doing, you will have to help them understand the cause of their behavior.

Observations you accept through your senses do not have any bearing on what happens in the future. That is, unless you let them. Your power to create is only limited by the boundaries you place on it. When you use your ability to form ideas and create an image of the future you want for yourself, and then impress that image onto the subconscious mind (fall in love with it), the energy that is flowing to and through you will move it into physical form.

Feelings are your barometer here. If it feels good, you are in the right vibration and will attract what feels good, thereby creating what is in harmony with those feelings. If you do not feel good, then your emotional involvement is off and you will be in harmony with what is off. You can make a course correction to feeling good by choosing to take in different thoughts and shifting your paradigm.

To help you take these principles and apply them to your own life, let's consider the following exercise:

- Start with a clean sheet of paper, and write down your ideal vision from Chapter 1. If you don't have a clear vision yet, that is okay, you can still do this exercise and benefit from it with any dream you have.

- Write down as much detail as possible for your vision or dream. For example, when, where, who else will be there, what does it smell like, look like, and sound like, etc.

- What will your life be like after your dreams come true? How will your life change?

- How are you feeling about it? Excited? Nervous? Jubilant? Write down everything you are feeling about it as if it is taking place right now.

- Take 5-10 minutes – no more – to visualize the picture you have written down and that you hold in your mind. Feel the emotions you're after, and put yourself in the picture.

- Repeat this exercise once a day at the same time, preferably in the same place.

The mind-body connection is extremely powerful, and must be understood to bring about long-term growth. If you want to change your life, you have to understand how you operate. This chapter has shown you how the conscious and subconscious mind work with the body to create paradigms and produce results. With this knowledge, you can start to reconstruct your paradigms to reach your goals. In the next chapter we will build upon this progress by exploring the six intellectual faculties we all possess. Understanding these faculties will help propel you towards living the life of your dreams.

Chapter 4

INTELLECTUAL PROWESS

"We are what we are according to our state of thinking."
~ Raymond Holliwell

We each have, in our conscious mind, five senses to help us understand the world: we can see, hear, smell, taste, and touch. These are amazing tools to experience our surroundings, and they are one means by which we enjoy our physical being. That being said, they are also very limited. By our conditioning, we often let them guide us and control our whole experience of the world, when they really only account for a small piece of it all.

In addition to these basic senses, we also have a higher skill set, which are our six intellectual faculties, or tools of the mind. They are:

1. Imagination
2. Intuition
3. Will
4. Memory
5. Reason
6. Perception

Everybody is endowed with these incredible gifts of Infinite Intelligence, but very few people have any understanding of how to use them to create the life of their dreams. Often, when people are using them, they are doing so unconsciously. They do not actually feel it, or even realize it occurred.

We all possess the same higher faculties, and when you put them to use, you can produce extraordinary results that separate you from the masses.

From an early age, children have been taught to respond to outside forces. They are constantly being told to listen up and look out. In other words, they are taught to only trust what comes through their senses. It is easy to see how this becomes the model for life, where only present results are taken into account. The truth is, all present results are nothing more than a record of past actions. Unfortunately, most people live their lives controlled by this paradigm of what has been.

As you understand more about your higher intellectual faculties, you will be able to use them much more effectively to your benefit and, if you choose, to guarantee phenomenal future performance.

Your highest function is thinking. In fact, it is what makes humans the highest form of creation on earth. With your mental toolbox, you will be able to enjoy the life of your dreams. Your own limits – those you place on yourself – are the only things standing in your way. Your potential is infinite and you are connected to an infinite source of supply. You have only scratched the surface of your capabilities.

It only takes a small amount of observation of the world around us to see the higher intellectual faculties in action. There are those people who formed an idea in their imagination, trusted their intuition, focused their will, remembered everything they needed, reasoned and discovered a better way, and perceived that it could in fact be done. They have brought us advancements in technology, access to goods and services, and have inspired others to do the same. They are just like you. You have the exact same source and the exact same mental toolbox. Your own mental limitations are the only difference. Let them go and let yourself shine!

While we need our senses to process the outside world, as they are perfect for doing so, we can see that there is a whole world we've been missing. Through the development and use of our higher faculties, creating and sustaining our own unique expression is much easier, and is a much greater gift to the world. Let's unpack these higher faculties in greater detail.

Imagination

> *"Our only limitation… lies in our development and use of our imagination."*
>
> *~ Napoleon Hill*

Imagination is where it all begins. Everything that exists in physical form first existed in the imagination, and so it is really created twice. The creative process, which is the basis for everything, starts with a fantasy (and fantasies are born in the imagination). If there were no imagination, there would be no creation. Your imagination is the spark that sets Source Energy into motion.

There are two aspects to the imaginative faculty:

1. *Synthetic imagination.* Synthetic imagination is the force that draws upon all manner of resources that already exist. It uses its power to rearrange and repurpose concepts, ideas, and plans into new and improved outputs. It is very useful, as it magnifies the power of various elements into a stronger, unified whole.

   This is what most of us use when working through ideas. We are tapping into the legacy of knowledge that has been left for us by every person who has walked the earth. Let's say you want to plant a garden. You are using synthetic imagination to select a location, lay out a workable plan, and use tools to dig, plant, and water. All of the resources necessary are already known, and you have put them to use in a new way to shape the garden you imagined.

2. *Creative imagination.* Creative imagination is the power of Infinite Intelligence. It can turn a simple thought into anything. It is this creative power that is tuned into the universal subconscious mind, and into the subconscious mind of others who are tuned into your vibration. Your focused desire gives it fuel and helps to draw the image out of your mind.

Intuition

> *"Freedom is from within."*
> ~ Frank Lloyd Wright

Intuition, your intuitive factor, is your ability to pick up vibrations and interpret those vibrations in your mind. It is your guide, your gut instinct, and is often referred to as your sixth sense. It is not a sense at all, but one of your higher faculties that you can develop and grow. With it, you can tune into another person's emotional and mental states. Intuition taps into the feeling of your future Self, your connection to Infinite Intelligence.

Practice using your intuition when you hear the voice inside – the one that you sometimes second-guess and dismiss. Begin to feel it and listen, knowing that intuition connects you to Source Energy, and that when it speaks it has something worth saying. Trust it when something feels right, and when something feels a little off. The more you practice using it, the more robust it becomes and the more you experience life on a more expansive level.

Will

> *"The true power of the gift of the will lies not in its ability to affect, but in its ability to attract."*
> ~ Sandy Gallagher

Will is the ability to focus and concentrate. In developing your will, you can learn to hold one image in your mind while excluding all outside distractions. With practice, your focus will get stronger.

The will is to the mind as a magnifying glass is to the sun – able to focus all of the light down to one point.

Combine will with the laws of vibration, transmutation, and attraction, and it is really your super power of attraction. You attract what you focus on and that which you are harmonious with. By developing and using the will, you speed up the vibration you are in and attract the exact image you hold in your subconscious mind.

There are many ways to train the will and improve your concentration. A very simple one is to focus on a small point on the wall opposite to where you are sitting in a room. As your mind wanders, simply bring it back to focus on the one point – do this over and over again. Eventually, you will become one with the point. With ongoing practice, you will be able to do this for extended periods of time and build your concentration so that you can apply it and focus on anything you wish.

Memory

> *"Past results are not a guarantee of future performance."*
>
> ~ Bob Proctor

Memory is how we encode, store, retain, and recall information or experiences. Like all of our higher faculties, it is perfect and can be strengthened with practice and exercise. No memory is "bad" or "good," but rather weak or strong. Being forgetful is not a function of recall, but rather the result of not having remembered something in the first place.

There are tools available to build and train your memory in various ways, like learning to memorize whole books or developing photographic recall of people's names. For most of them, the process involves association – usually ridiculous association – that creates pictures in your mind, which are very easy to remember. For example, if you want to remember someone's name, you can use a substitute word technique based on the sounds of the name and then associate those to facial features or physical characteristics that are most prominent. Using Jay Billig, you might picture a blue <u>jay</u> with a duck<u>bill</u> chomping its leg. That may be enough, but if not, you might notice blue eyes and a quacking voice to add to the ridiculous picture. You can do this with anyone and anything. If you decide to strengthen your memory by creating pictures and associations, you will quickly amaze yourself with your newfound skills.

Reason

> *"Realize the perspective from which reality is your servant and not your master."*
>
> ~ Story Waters

Reason is the tool that allows us to think. We have the ability to originate thoughts and coalesce them to form ideas. The superpower strength it gives us is our ability to choose. We have the power of self-observation, and we have the ability to create new ideas of how we can do things better the next time, continually improving ourselves and our results.

It is with reason that we can also choose which thoughts to think and which ideas to take in. Developing your reasoning faculty will also help you better decode which thoughts are positive and which are negative, thereby focusing on the positive and creating ideas on why or how things can be done. A great exercise any individual (or even better, any group) can use to develop their reasoning factor goes like this:

- When you are dealing with something that seems impossible on the surface, write out the big idea on the top of a piece of paper and put a line under it. Draw another line down the middle of the page, creating a "T" with the first line.

- In the space that is created on the left column of the "T" draw a giant "X" to fill the entire space. In this column goes every reason why the thing cannot be done. Since there is no place to write it down, it is not possible to even entertain the idea of it. Every time someone offers a reason why it cannot be done, say, "NEXT!" and skip that reason.

- Be open and listen for all the reasons why it can be done and in the column on the right, write down every idea and reason that fits the bill. As you or the group engage in the exercise, there are no ideas that are too out there – consider all your options. Continue to brainstorm "yes ideas" and continue to "NEXT!" all the "no ideas" until you come up with what is workable to achieve the objective you identified at the top of the page. Finally, commit to execute on the ideas that are laid out in front of you and get to work on it.

Perception

> *"When we change the way we look at things, the things we look at change."*
>
> ~ Wayne Dyer

Perception is our perspective – our point of view or how we see things. With this faculty, we can change the way we look at any situation we are involved in, whether we see it as positive or negative. You can recognize that there is always another perspective. When you run into obstacles, you may be able to easily overcome them by simply shifting your perspective on how you view them.

Your perception of something affects whether it shows up as big or small. Take a problem that feels insurmountable and write it on a small piece of paper. When you hold it in your hand, you see it as something huge that you are faced with and it weighs on you. Now place it on the table in front of you and step away to look at the piece of paper from a distance. Do you see the problem or just the paper? If you are still seeing the problem, go to the other side of the table and try a different view, a different perspective. Eventually, you won't be able to see the problem, and it won't seem so huge anymore. Shifting your perspective shifts the whole world.

Putting Them Together

All of your higher intellectual faculties – your mental muscles, or mind toolbox – work together to make you the powerhouse of the planet. Your ability to think is what sets you apart from the rest of the animal world. When you understand the power locked up inside you, it will become clear that you really have been given the keys to the kingdom. And when you begin to use your muscles, there is literally nothing you cannot achieve.

The mind works in a cycle, in rhythm. Most people's standard rhythm goes something like this:

- You look at your current results and let them register in your conscious mind, which causes you to think.

- This thinking is then impressed (completely by accident because of a lack of conscious awareness) onto the subconscious mind, which produces a feeling.

- This feeling automatically causes actions that are in the same vibration as the feeling, and the actions produce results – the same results.

- This rhythm is the story told by the vast majority of people. It is how they keep getting the same results over and over again, year after year.

It takes courage to look at yourself objectively and observe your results in a way that a stranger might see them. Be courageous and get in the driver's seat!

When you do this, you will observe things you do not want. Welcome that feeling of dissatisfaction and then ask yourself: What do I want? Think thoughts and ideas that will form the image of what you do want. This is how you put yourself into a new rhythm, by inserting new thoughts from the place of your goals. Here's what that looks like:

- Look at your current results and let them register in your conscious mind, causing you to think.

- This thinking is then impressed (purposely because your conscious awareness has been elevated) onto the subconscious mind, which produces a feeling.

- This feeling automatically causes actions that are in the same vibration as the feeling, and the actions produce results – measurably new results.

- Observe the new results and start again to think new thoughts of what could be done to make it even better.

These new thoughts cause the feelings, which cause the actions, which produce the results – new results in harmony with the vibration of your feelings about your new thoughts. This new rhythm has you continually observing new results and adding new thoughts that create ideas to improve upon them. You are now controlling the outside world – you are the driver of your own bus. With a growing understanding of your intellectual faculties and the picture of your mind, you are now able to see yourself in what seems like a totally different mirror, and you are creating the life of your dreams.

Once you grasp the power of your thoughts and your vibrations, and experience your improved results, you can begin to trust yourself more and more. In turn, it will contribute to developing a strong, confident self-image that will help you achieve more goals and actualize more dreams. We will explore this self-image more in the next chapter.

Chapter 5

PERSONAL RENDERINGS ILLUMINATED

*"To learn to trust your inner senses
is to learn to trust your Self."*
~ Story Waters

Your conscious mind is the realm of your intellectual faculties and how you see yourself from the outside – while the full-scale model of you rendered in full color is contained in the subconscious mind.

There are many deeply embedded factors that hold us back. Now is the time to recognize that you are a creative beauty, and that everything you have done up until now has prepared you to be the star in the movie that is your life. You get to write your own ticket, and create your own script.

It is not possible to overstate how important self-image is to the life you create. Not only is self-image all-important, it can always be improved. It is what you believe about yourself that determines everything that you are able to do, and also every limitation you are up against.

We all have two mental images: one that we see reflected back to us from the mirror and one that we hold internally in our minds.

Your inner self-image is the deep programming of your mind with a perception of who you are, what you are to yourself and the world, and also what you are worth. It is like a valve that controls everything that comes into your life, including your level of well-being and abundance.

You also have an outer self-image, which is how you show up in the world. It is the way you carry yourself, the way you interact with people, and the way you walk, talk, and dress. It is the outer expression of your inner self-image.

The results that show up on the outside are a direct reflection of the image you have of yourself on the inside. Your subconscious mind is where you hold your self-image, which then guides what the world sees of you. It is possible to change your self-image, to improve upon it, but you are the only person who can do anything about it. Through visualizing yourself as you want to be, you get to decide what you look like inside and out.

Being the physical manifestation of Pure Source Energy, there is an image of perfection deep in your consciousness. The more you learn about who you really are, the more you will be able to see that image unfold and decide if you are happy with it or not.

You can continually move in the direction of perfection, improving your self-image and the image you project out to the world. The perfection of your spiritual DNA is unwavering and the more you understand about yourself, the more you will see it in yourself.

You are set up for greatness – to magnify the good within you. Recognize it, and claim it. Your image of yourself is the only thing stopping you. Living the life of your dreams happens when you create rather than compete. And when you create, having fun and working become the same thing. You will inspire the people you work with, and they will be inspired by you. Cooperation is key and helping everybody be the best they can be will prove to you that competition is ineffective. Only through creation do we all benefit.

Take Action: Believe Your Way to Your Goals

We keep coming back to your beliefs. What do you believe about yourself and what you are capable of achieving? Imagine there is a movie of your life as you have been living it. What is your role? Are you the lead character or a member of the supporting cast? As your mental image forms, ask yourself if your beliefs are serving you in your desire to move forward, or if they are holding you back. How you see yourself, and what you believe deep down, is the way you show up in your movie. Do you like what you see?

It is very helpful to write down the story of your life to help you objectively examine it and gain an understanding of what beliefs are at the root of the image you project to the world. Include important people, places, and events that have shaped you and continue to have an influence on you. Use lots of detail and include how you felt at various times throughout your life. Make sure to show times when you have been very happy and proud, in addition to the times that were more challenging. Once you have written your script, step back and read it as though you are looking at the life of a total stranger. What is your favorite part? What would make the sequel even better?

Create two lists of all the things you see yourself doing in your current script. The first list will be positive, productive things and the second will be negative, non-productive things. Be honest with yourself and recognize that your self-image is impacting your life.

Now take the second list and next to each negative activity, separately write out the positive version (the opposite) of each one. The goal is to destroy that negative list. Burn it or shred it. Or shred it AND burn it. Obliterate the limited image you hold of yourself and open up to what is possible. As you do it, imagine that the positive things you wrote down are now what you believe.

Now the real fun starts! It is your turn to create the screenplay of your wonderful life. Dig into your imagination and, using what you already know to be positive in your life, write the story of your life. This is the story of the life of your dreams. Get vivid and playful. Don't be shy about letting your star shine! This is YOUR movie. You are the star and every supporting character is there because they love being a part of your life. As you write your screenplay, feel yourself living it. Remember, what you believe internally is what you create in your life and in the world. The world is ready for you – the best version of you!

You have learned a lot about what makes you tick, about what has been holding you back, and about your spiritual perfection. In very short order, you will get to see what has been going on since the beginning of time, and will understand how you and your entire world are governed by a set of rules that completely level the playing field. Learning about these laws will help you grow and continue to create the life of your dreams.

Part II

LAWS TO LIVE: THE UNBREAKABLE RULES OF THE GAME

"There are really only two stars in every one of our dramas: The Universe (and its unfailing principles) and you."

~ Mike Dooley

To this point, you have learned about the inner workings of both yourself and your marvelous mind. This section is all about the inner workings of everything that exists, seen and unseen, including you.

Throughout Part II, you will get to take a walk with Katie and Jack as they experience the laws of life. Put yourself in their shoes and notice how you too are experiencing these laws every moment of every day.

Jack and Katie have known each other for a while. They went to school together but came from vastly different backgrounds. Somehow, though, it is like they were cut from the same cloth and it has been that way since they met. People often confuse them for a couple because they are so close that they finish each other's sentences. They both have incredible groups of friends, some in common, that they feel deeply connected to. They love to do things together and support each other's growth. They have become friendly within their individual families, colleagues, and teams. They take great pleasure in seeing each other do well and thrive.

Universal laws are always operating, wherever you look and wherever you go. They exist in the background all the time and in full view as well. They affect every aspect of your life, from the dust that collects on your furniture to galaxies beyond the edge of space. These laws oversee literally everything that we know about and everything not yet revealed to us. They operate with every person, every moment, everywhere. There is no escaping these laws in life, and yet few people are even aware that these laws exist, much less that they shape their very journey. These laws are as basic as gravity, always on and inescapable. These laws govern gravity itself as well.

Everybody gets the same deal in life. Understanding these laws will help you see that life is 100% fair, 100% of the time (or 100% unfair if you choose to see it that way.) There is no advantage given to any one individual in the way the universe operates, but how they use those circumstances often separates wonderful success from great failure. Life is completely neutral and does not care if you are living on pennies a month or are a multi-billionaire. Either way, your decisions, which are operating by these laws, got you where you are today. The game is the same for everybody. No matter who you are, these same rules apply. The infinite potential of each individual is exactly the same.

You have the option to ignore them, learn about them academically, or dive in deep and experience them as you go. Most people ignore them, unaware or unmotivated to understand what occurs around them. In that case, they often feel as if life is happening to them. The academic approach is summed up in the attitude "hmmm… good to know." But that does not actually result in some specific internalization and inevitable action.

However, true and lasting transformation is recognized when you really understand these laws on a deep level and use them to guide you through life. As you gain an understanding of them, and see how you and the entire world you live in are governed by them, you will be able to seemingly mold them. You are not actually molding them, but rather choosing the way you experience them.

It is like turning a light on in a dark room – pure enlightenment. You will then understand your power to choose ANYTHING you desire. Your wish is the command of the Universe.

Chapter 6

LAW OF ONENESS

Everything is connected to everything else. What we think, say, do and believe will have a corresponding effect on others and the universe around us.

Another way of saying this is that we are all one. We are all literally one being, manifested in infinite ways, and as such, the thoughts of every person, the actions of every creature, and the movement of every celestial body are elements of the One. When you see another person you are literally seeing yourself. When you touch a puppy, you are literally touching a version of yourself reflected back at you. When you smell a flower or breakfast cooking, you are literally smelling yourself. The sound of a bird's song is you hearing yourself. And when you feel joy for your friend you are celebrating yourself. Likewise, when something you encounter really stinks, it's you. Everything is you and you are everything.

We are conditioned to being separate, so this may seem drastic at first. The impression of separateness allows us to find fault and blame people and conditions outside of ourselves for our own life. When you find a reason to fault or blame another, it is really finding fault with yourself. When you understand that we are all one, you can begin to dismantle the illusion that is separation. When this illusion melts away, cooperation is the natural state of being. You are then able to experience yourself present with every person you encounter. Thus, their gain is your gain.

We are taught all about our differences, and value that which makes us unique. Oneness does not diminish our uniqueness, quite the opposite in fact. We are each a unique manifestation of Spirit in Motion, a perfect expression of One Source, directly linked to every other perfect expression of Itself. This is observable at every scale: one marker on a whole strand of DNA, one cell in a whole organ, one organ in a whole creature, one petal on a whole flower, one person in a whole family or group, one class in a whole school, one cloud in a whole atmosphere, one planet in a whole solar system, one star in a whole galaxy, one galaxy among billions in one region of the universe. The scientific and psychological explanation of this concept is called a holon, which is a whole and complete entity (the lungs, for example) that exists within another whole and complete entity (the body), and is itself made up of whole and complete entities (cells). The methodology is different and the conclusions are exactly the same – one Infinite Source and infinite individual expressions of Itself.

Jack noticed a rash on his stomach. It would not go away with any remedy he had in his medicine cabinet. So, he went to see his doctor to try to get to the bottom of it. She looked at it and diagnosed it, prescribing a cream for him to use on it. He did as she said for a couple of weeks, but it did not go away. His response was to make an appointment with a dermatologist to get some answers. The dermatologist identified the rash as something different than his family physician had and sent Jack home with another prescription. After a few more weeks, with the rash still there, Jack told Katie about it, who recommended he go to see a holistic practitioner with which she was familiar. Jack went, and through the use of applied kinesiology (also called muscle testing) she was able to identify that Jack had developed a sensitivity or allergy to soy. He immediately removed it from his diet and watched the rash disappear within just a few days.

By tapping into the energy of All That Is, the holistic practitioner helped Jack like none of the physicians could.

Chapter 7
LAW OF VIBRATION

Everything in the Universe moves, vibrates, and travels in circular patterns, the same principles of vibration in the physical world apply to our thoughts, feelings, desires and wills in the Etheric world. Each sound, thing, and even thought has its own vibrational frequency, unique unto itself.

This law is of utmost importance because nearly all of the other laws here are expressions of it. So gaining an understanding of the law of vibration can lead to more easily understanding and using the entire rulebook.

One of the easiest ways to understand the law of vibration is through music. When voices are in unison, or in certain harmonies, it can move us to tears. Strings on an instrument, when made to vibrate, produce a particular sound, as well as overtones related to the particular tuning. When two adjacent strings are tuned to the same pitch, plucking one will cause both to vibrate. Music is called the universal language because it causes us to vibrate along with the instruments and musicians. When some music plays it compels us to dance like nobody's watching.

There is nothing that is still in all of the universe. Everything is in a constant state of motion and change, increasing or decreasing its vibration. At a molecular level this can be easily observed, and when doing so also alters the motion. There is a direct correlation between a thing's material state and its speed of vibration. The states of water demonstrate this well: Ice moves very slowly, liquid water at a moderate rate, and water vapor at a higher frequency.

Another way to observe the law of vibration in action is being in love. You meet someone who you really connect with, on an emotional level, and there is nothing that can keep you apart. You are magnetically charged, drawn to one another, vibrating at the same frequency, and it feels amazing! When people become parents, they find themselves in baby-love too, drawn together with their child, creating a bonding frequency that is impossible to break.

Our thoughts and feelings are also vibrating, and it is the vibrational frequency of our feelings that guide the actions of our bodies as a vehicle of the subconscious mind. Whatever vibration you are feeling will be what gets expressed through the body. If you are in a positive vibrational frequency, you will get positive results. The vibration of the subconscious mind, what we refer to as feelings, is what will be expressed, and when it is expressed, more of the same vibration will be brought forth from the creative ether. Your vibration literally controls everything you do and every result that you are getting.

Katie invited Jack to go with her to a party put on by some mutual friends. Jack was in a real funk and said he didn't want to go. He was feeling bummed out about something that had happened at work earlier in the day. Katie pressed him and he reluctantly agreed to meet her there, even though he really felt like wallowing in his misery alone. When he arrived, Katie greeted him with a big hug and he could see with all the laughter and dancing that people were having a great time. A story told by one of his friends got him to crack a smile and once that door was opened, he couldn't help but laugh out loud. Before long, he was cutting up and shaking his body along with the rest of the revelers, decidedly out of his funk and in the spirit of celebration.

In short, he was vibrating at a higher, more positive frequency.

Chapter 8

LAW OF ACTION

Must be employed in order for us to manifest things on earth. We must engage in actions that support our thoughts, dreams, emotions and words.

Actions are always taken from whatever vibration you are in. Since your body is what you use to take any action, and your body is a vehicle of the mind, consciously aligning what feels good with your actions will set you up for greater success.

The first step in any manifestation is a thought, whether it be simple or grand. It is our ability to think that is the foundation of all things that become a reality. Begin with a thought: think it, dream it, feel it, speak it. Once the mind is engaged, Source Energy immediately begins to formulate the means by which it will come into physical being.

Continually impressing the image of what you want to manifest onto your subconscious or feeling mind will set up the belief that it is already here and cause you to vibrate in harmony with what it is you are creating. This will also cause your body to take action to support your dream.

A lot of people draw up really great plans for new homes or renovations to an existing place, even creating digital renderings of what it will look like when it is all complete. However, they may never get moving enough to build it. The plans are perfect, with every detail spelled out and every consideration made for the lives of potential occupants, but unless someone decides to take action, the plans just sit there looking pretty.

Action is absolutely critical to the manifestation of anything. If you say you want something but don't impress the belief that it is yours to have, it will be nothing more than a daydream. Once you believe it and take action toward its attainment, it must happen. There is a creative power that is flowing to and through you. When your feelings are in alignment with the thoughts you have originated about what it is that you want, your actions will automatically lead it to you. Your actions are a direct reflection of your beliefs and feelings, and your results will prove it every time.

Jack had been talking about running a marathon for years; often saying it was on his bucket list. The farthest he had ever run, though, was about 3 miles, and that was back in high school. He was all talk and no action. One day Katie, now fairly sick of hearing about his some-day marathon, challenged him to quit talking and get off the couch. He decided right then and there that "some day" would come soon, since their city hosted a marathon in just 6 months. He got out his phone and registered for it on the spot. He had set his goal and now he had to do something about it. The next day he started with a short jog of a few blocks in the neighborhood and it seriously wiped him out! "What was I thinking?" he wondered. He carried on, even though there were some days where he wished he had never heard of a bucket list. After a few weeks, he was running a few miles at a time, and by the time a few months had passed he was doing so very easily. He joined a training group and learned from seasoned athletes, who taught him all about the best regimen to follow. When race day came, Katie was there to cheer him on and they were both proud of what he had accomplished using persistent action.

There lies the law of action, which propelled Jack to complete a lifelong goal.

Chapter 9

LAW OF CORRESPONDENCE

> *This Universal Law states that the principles or laws of physics that explain the physical world, energy, Light, vibration, and motion have their corresponding principles in the etheric or universe – "As above, so below."*

Considering that All is One and everything vibrates, connections across all realms of existence is a natural state for Source Energy. You could call it a known unknown. This is right up there with dark matter – we know it exists because of its effect on gravity, but it has yet to be revealed to scientists. For our human observations, we can see the beautiful patterns in galaxies, nebulae, and other celestial wonders like solar flares and supernovae. When placed alongside our creative power, imagining the One at work having fun with its unfolding is proof in action.

And when the Source is certain and infinite, truly anything is possible. Just as anything that can be measured or felt has its opposite in this plane, so it is at any level of conscious awareness.

For us, the way we show up in the world is a direct reflection of what we hold in our subconscious mind. Everything that resides in the subconscious – beliefs, paradigms, and self-image – is the source of our vibration and corresponds to our physical presence. When you acquire anything (like a new pair of shoes, jeans, or a car, for example) you begin to notice all kinds of people with the same style. Your vibration on the inside had you choose that thing and now that you have it, you're tuned into it on the outside all around.

Our five physical senses – see, hear, smell, taste, touch – are the means by which we are connected to and take in the world around us. These senses, as well as our mental faculties, provide a direct connection for us to Source energy. Every means by which we experience life is an expression of Source, and so it is that Source experiences itself by and through all things and us. Infinite Power has infinite ways to experience itself on this plane and all other planes.

Katie noticed that she felt physically affected when she spent any time with her friend, Jo, who always seemed to have a complaint about someone or something. One day, after they had had a visit, Jack asked Katie if she was feeling ok, if she might not be sick. She said she would be fine and that she just had an overdose of Jo. "Funny thing," she said. "I was hanging out with Jo and now I just feel kinda weird. Usually I can brush it off, but this time I seem to have gotten myself all tied up in a knot." Jack pointed out that she hit the nail on the head: she got HERSELF all tied up. Once she heard that, she was able to switch her perspective and think of all the reasons she really likes Jo instead of what was bugging her about their relationship.

Following the law of correspondence allowed Katie to shift her vantage point about Jo.

Chapter 10

LAW OF CAUSE AND EFFECT

Nothing happens by chance or outside the Universal Laws. Every Action (including thought) has a reaction or consequence — "We reap what we sow."

As with the law of vibration, the law of cause and effect is a primary one. Ralph Waldo Emerson called it "the law of laws" because everything that exists can be traced back through it to identify its source. Isaac Newton also identified it: "For every action, there is an equal and opposite reaction."

There is no such thing as coincidence. What might appear to be such is the effect of our thoughts and actions, which have caused those "coincidences." One very simple example of this law as it plays out in our daily lives is when you think of a friend or family member and then they call you later that day.

When the thoughts and actions that we are engaged in are positive and life-affirming for everybody who is touched by them, we get a reaction from people and the universal mind that is positive and life-affirming as well. Let's say you have a meeting scheduled and everybody shows up on time and ready to participate fully. You then have a very productive meeting, and a post-meeting task list that people want to take on for the betterment of the whole group. When you engage in creative commerce and set up your dealings with others as win-win situations, then win-win situations will be exactly the reaction that comes forth for you. This is true for other times as well.

Holidays are a great time to experience the law of cause and effect. When food is everywhere with lots of snacks, huge meals, and ample desserts, nearly everybody has experienced being so full of food that they feel like they're going to burst. Your insatiable appetite was the cause, and an uncomfortable stomachache is the result, usually obvious only after the fact.

With a natural state of well-being, when dis-ease shows up, it can be traced to a specific cause which might be a one time event or a lifetime of inputs to create the effect that is being experienced in the body. As it is with the body, in any place, group or situation, when an effect is observed, the cause is right around the corner. While it is important that we be able to identify the cause of any particular effect, unless it is a very positive one, we would be best to spend our time creating causes that will produce effects to our liking. Think of what you do want, and keep thinking about it. Feel good having the experience before it shows up, and then celebrate it when it does.

Katie and Jack have a mutual friend, Al, who lives across the country. They usually make a point of getting together once a year or so to keep their connection going. This year, when they made plans to meet up, Al had to cancel due to a family situation that came up. All of them were disappointed and kept thinking of alternate dates they could arrange to be together, but none surfaced. Meanwhile, Jack and Katie had the occasion to do a weekend away in Chicago where they were having such a good time that they decided to extend their trip by a couple of days. When they went to lunch on Monday, they looked across the room and whom did they see but Al! They were all very pleasantly surprised. Turns out Al had come to Chicago for a business trip to visit a client and would be there until late on Tuesday night – the same schedule as Katie and Jack. They also discovered he was staying in the same hotel! They would get to have their togetherness after all.

And so, the above story demonstrates the law of cause and effect at work.

Chapter 11

LAW OF COMPENSATION

The Universal Law is the Law of Cause and Effect applied to blessings and abundance that are provided for us. The visible effects of our deeds are given to us in gifts, money, inheritances, friendships, and blessings.

As with the "law of laws" and the law of vibration, this one is primary. There is no escaping it as you work your way through life. This law might be misunderstood to be a kind of score-keeper or holder of a universal cash machine. It is important to understand that there is an infinite supply of abundance, and the only thing keeping anything from us is our own limiting beliefs. Not only is the Source infinite, but it also wants to expand itself by and through us.

The thoughts we think and what is impressed upon our subconscious mind – by experiences early in life, accidentally or on purpose – is what we feel and believe, and thus how we are compensated from all the riches of All That Is. The level of compensation we receive for anything we are doing in life is in direct proportion to the need for what we are doing, our ability to do it, and how difficult it is to replace us. As long as there are people willing to trade money or other services for what you are offering, it can be said there is a need for what you are doing. Your ability to do it is the skill you hone over time, and when you get really good at doing your thing, you become very difficult to replace.

When you are the cause of being a friend, the effect is having friends in your life. When you are the cause of giving money away or spending it on quality services, the effect is having more than enough money to give away and spend on people providing quality services.

We all experience blessings and abundance at seemingly different scales, and when we are thankful for them, more must come to us. The act of giving thanks comes naturally from the place of having the thing you are thankful for, and when you are in that vibration, you attract more of it to you. There is an opportunity to find the blessings in any situation and create more of that in our lives. The more we are thankful, the more it sets us up to believe in the abundance of the Universe and provide further proof of it all around. Being more thankful will create many more reasons to be thankful; we will see these showing up everywhere we turn.

Jack felt totally stuck in his job and was looking for a major change of scenery. He was in the software development industry and had set a goal to start his own company. He contacted colleagues that he had enjoyed working with over the years and invited them to join his new team. A dozen of them took him up on it, creating a deep field of expertise and commitment to serving their customers. He and one other person who was particularly good at sales went about finding clients. They offered a turnkey service for clients who needed that level of service, and a menu of individualized services for those who didn't need the whole enchilada. Soon, they had to bring on more developers so they could meet the demand for what they were doing. By the time a year was up, Jack was earning three times what he had made as an employee, and enjoying every minute of it.

Jack shows us that, so long as you create value, you'll always reap the benefits with the law of compensation.

Chapter 12

LAW OF ATTRACTION

Demonstrates how we create the things, events, and people that come into our lives. Our thoughts, feelings, words, and actions produce energies, which in turn attract like energies. Negative energies attract negative energies and positive energies attract positive energies.

This law is a direct relation to the Law of Vibration. When you are in a positive vibration, you put out positive thoughts and actions, which attract positive energy to yourself. In fact, as you are putting out any thought or feeling, uttering any word or engaging in any action, the vibration of it is matched and you are instantly filled with more of the same energy

There is no delay in this vibrationally, but it can be confusing because the manifestation of positive results usually has a delay. When we use negative words, thoughts, feelings, and actions, the reaction is usually instantaneous, like a slap in the face reminding us how the universe works. Pause, observe, and take on positive feelings to reset the momentum you really want to have in your life.

To tap into the power of the law of attraction, your best tools are a very clear, definite goal that you are totally passionate about; asking for it and believing it is yours to have or to be, taking steps in its direction with faith that you cannot fail, and giving thanks for and celebrating it before, during, and after you magnetize it to you.

It is important to note that we are the originators of our own thoughts about any situation we may find ourselves in. When we think positive thoughts and repetitively impress them upon the subconscious mind, we must take actions that are positive as well. By continually thinking positive thoughts, uttering positive words, feeling a positive vibration, and taking positive actions, positive energies will be the norm and you will have more and more positive energy that is attracted into your life. Once you have attracted this positive energy, it will be easier to create more positive results.

Katie was ready to have a boyfriend in her life and Jack was ready to stop being confused for that guy. Katie decided to set the intention to attract someone who would be a good fit so she created a list of all the best qualities of each of the guys she had dated in the past, and also those she had never before experienced. She asked herself, "What does it feel like to experience all of these qualities in one person?" "What would it feel like to give myself fully to being with someone and being fully appreciated?" As the days went by, she kept asking the same questions and putting herself in the space to actually feel those things. After a few weeks had passed, she was at a gallery for the opening of an exhibition by one of her friends when she was introduced to Marco, the friend of a friend. They hit it off talking about photography and food, which led to a dinner date the next day and a walk in the park a few days after that, and…

Now you see how powerful the law of attraction can be.

Chapter 13

LAW OF PERPETUAL TRANSMUTATION OF ENERGY

All persons have within them the power to change the conditions of their lives. Higher vibrations consume and transform lower ones; thus, each of us can change the energies in our lives by understanding the Universal Laws and applying the principles in such a way as to effect change.

That's a mouthful no matter how you read it. Transmutation means, "the action of changing or the state of being changed into another form." Everything is in a constant state of motion and everything, known and unknown, is in a constant state of transformation. One form of energy is fuel for another, higher form. There is no death, only transformation. Death as we think of it is a repurposing of molecules that will continue to contain all of the encoded information the entity had before transformation. A seed cannot remain a seed for a plant to become a plant, and a plant cannot remain a plant for food to become food. We live in an ocean of motion with nothing becoming everything and everything becoming nothing.

Dr. Wayne Dyer very simply and eloquently demonstrated this with only seven letters:

NO WHERE uses the same letters in the same order as NOW HERE. A slight shift of the space and the experience is completely transformed, yet remains one and the same. That is to say, all energy (and everything is energy) is always here, present, and accounted for, as well as completely hidden with everything inside.

All energy and all knowledge has always been and will always be. Nothing is created or destroyed, only transformed by becoming the next highest version of itself. Picture an acorn that contains everything necessary to become a sapling and then a giant of the forest, finally transforming itself into fuel. The way to do anything at all has always been here, and only became known as someone sought to know it and thus put it in motion, raising their vibration and conscious awareness of that thing. When one person becomes aware of a thing, all of humanity has access to the higher vibration and awareness.

The way to build a skyscraper or put a satellite into orbit around the planet has always been here. It was not until someone had the idea and then turned that idea into a burning desire that they were able to raise their conscious awareness enough to discover it. Then they were finally able to see the thing they had been seeking, and in short order it became common knowledge, shared with the whole Universal Mind.

It is by this law that we know that anything is possible and that thoughts become things. A thought to be or become something more is the first step into a higher vibration. As the thought is repeated and it becomes a belief, it spurs action on the part of the believer. Actions based on belief will cause the transformation of the One Source to produce the result of the thing that was the subject of the original thought.

Jack had a patch of dirt in his back yard that he decided to turn into a vegetable garden. He didn't have a clue what to do or where to start. Upon doing a little bit of research, he discovered that the soil contains the magic for successful gardening, and that he wanted to grow everything organically, avoiding any chemicals or commercial plant food. He found out that to have healthy soil, there needs to be a lot of compost and humus to amend it with, so he started a compost operation with food scraps, grass clippings, and leaves. All those things he used to throw away were now being transformed into the rich black fuel for his garden. By the end of the season, he was growing so much food he could not possibly use all of it. His thought about creating a garden had more than grown to maturity and every element of the cycle he had set up was contributing to its continued existence. Vegetables became food for him and his circle; leftovers, stems, and scraps became compost, which became fuel for more plants, more food, and on and on…

Such a remarkable example of how, as energy, trash and treasure are one and the same.

Chapter 14

LAW OF RELATIVITY

Each person will receive a series of problems (Tests of Initiation/ Lessons) for the purpose of strengthening the light within; each of these tests/lessons will be a challenge and remain connected to our hearts when proceeding to solve the problems. This law also teaches us to compare our problems to others' problems in order to put things into proper perspective. No matter how bad we perceive our situation to be, there is always someone who is in a worse position. It's all relative..

All of the laws are interconnected and interdependent. Your level of awareness and understanding, and thus, ability to choose something different for your experience of life is what makes the difference.

Everything, all energy, just is until it is measured in relation to something else. All things, by their nature, are only measurable because they are being compared to other things. In the observable world, we have the ability to compare things with each other and they are only valid within the context of that particular moment or comparison. If you are getting a haircut, you might observe that your hair has gotten really long and needs a trim. It is only in relation to your freshly cut hair that you can be aware of that. For the person who wears their hair long enough to require combing, yours might be short no matter what length you have it.

We all use comparisons all the time – sometimes to our benefit and sometimes against ourselves. It is natural to compare ourselves to others, but it is what we do with it that makes the difference. For example, if you see that someone does something better than you, that they have really mastered it, you can either react to it and see yourself as not good enough, and be jealous of their abilities, or you can respond to it and be inspired to do what you do really well at the level of mastery.

Money, income, and prosperity are also very relative. If you earn minimum wage in the United States, you are wealthy compared to a person earning $100 per month in Tanzania. And if you earn $100,000 per month it is a pittance relative to the income Oprah rakes in every day. This law is important to understand because, as you can see, if everything just is, you can stop comparing yourself to anyone but yourself and choose ANY version of what is.

The most recognizable reference to relativity is courtesy of the scientist, Albert Einstein (1879-1955). In his special theory of relativity, Einstein gives us the equation $E=mc^2$ or Energy = mass x the speed of light^2, which is used to understand some special observations of the world. He went on to come up with a general theory of relativity, which is still being tested to gain a deeper understanding. As with the other aspects of relativity discussed here, it is the observer that determines much of what is so, and the observer has an effect on the object of its attention.

Katie was asked to put together a dinner party to benefit the local food bank. It would be limited to 50 guests who would each pay $1,000 for the dinner that would be prepared by volunteer celebrity chefs. The venue was the terrace of a hilltop estate overlooking the city, which was also donated along with all of the tables, plates, flowers, etc. that would be necessary. She had an assistant working with her leading up to the event who at the last minute got sick and could not be there the day it was to take place. She had to think fast and remembered a young man she had met at the food bank who had *told her that he had dreamed of attending the event. Katie found him and asked if he could step in to help. He jumped at the chance and showed up in his one pair of black pants and a clean white shirt. He was so helpful, doing anything and everything that Katie asked of him. After all the guests had left and the place was cleaned up, Katie, immensely grateful for all he had done, gave him $100 for his help, which was all the money she had with her. He was shocked! He said he had never earned more than $50 in a day before and it was like he had won the lottery being able to be at the event AND double his earnings.*

The law of relativity just goes to show how exceeding expectations can create monumental results.

Chapter 15

LAW OF POLARITY

Everything is on a continuum and has an opposite. We can suppress and transform undesirable thoughts by concentrating on the opposite pole. It is the law of mental vibrations.

Even if the name is new to you, the law of polarity is one that we observe all the time in our lives and in the world around us. We understand it as the opposites up and down, black and white, hot and cold, young and old, positive and negative: It is not possible to have one without the other. It is by the experience of death that we learn to appreciate life and through heartache that we are able to fully embrace love. In the physical world, this is pretty obvious and most of us stop there. We see the opposites out there and think they are fixed; that they both have control over our lives.

Hold up a coffee cup between two people and have them describe exactly what they each see. You will get very different descriptions of the same object. It works with a coin, or a book, or pretty much anything in life. Each person is seeing what they see from their perspective, relative to their position and the thing itself. There is no right or wrong, good or bad. They are both right in what they describe and the thing has not changed.

We have all heard the proclamation, "that's just the way it is," when someone is faced with a difficult question and there appears to be a lot more problems than solutions. Understanding the law of polarity and applying it allows us to see that there is an opposite to everything, and if we choose to focus on the positive ("I know there must be a way") rather than the negative ("It can't be done") the solutions will come. This law shows us that in every perceived failure there is a success.

Since there is an opposite to everything, we can observe the results in our lives, and if they are negative or undesirable, identify the opposite and focus on it to purposely impress what it is we want onto the subconscious mind. So, while on the surface this law is obvious and easy, it is also the law that allows us to readily transform ourselves into what we most desire. There is unlimited potential in every moment of life and we get to choose which version of it we want to experience.

Jack decided he wanted to buy a home. However, he had been self-employed for a about a year and quickly discovered that traditional lenders wouldn't give him the time of day much less a mortgage. Hearing "no" over and over had him doubting whether his dream could be realized. Katie stepped in and helped him take a broader view of the situation by asking, "how CAN you do it? There must be a way," she said. So he asked himself, "If I didn't think this was impossible what would I do?" Together they made a list of all the ways they could think of to buy a home without a lender: Cash, rent to own, seller financing, inheritance, etc. Then he started looking. Sure enough, without having to look very far at all, he found the perfect 2 bedroom home in the exact location where he most wanted to live where the seller was willing to carry a note at a great rate for 5 years. He made an offer, worked out the deal with the seller, and now is enjoying all the benefits of owning the home he had pictured just a few months before.

It is truly mesmerizing how we understand one thing in the context of another, illustrating the value of the law of polarity.

Chapter 16

LAW OF RHYTHM

Everything vibrates and moves to certain rhythms. These rhythms establish seasons, cycles, stages of development, and patterns. Each cycle reflects the regularity of the Universe. Masters know how to rise above negative parts of a cycle by never getting too excited or allowing negative things to penetrate their consciousness.

It is the law of Rhythm that governs the ebb and flow of all energy that exists. The yin and the yang in eastern philosophy is its imbedded operation in All That Is. Both exist simultaneously, yet independently and interdependently. The phases of the moon, sunrise and sunset, rising and falling of the tide are all physical examples of the law of rhythm.

There are rhythms to your experience of life as well, like a pendulum swinging between levels of love present in your life. By understanding the rhythm of life and seeing it as you go through it, you can appreciate the full spectrum of life from any point in the swing. In the ocean, when you resist the tide, it will knock you down or pull you under. If you rise with the tide, it will keep you above water and even deliver you safely to shore. Go with the flow by focusing on the good that is on its way as the pendulum swings down, knowing and trusting in your heart that it must be coming in the upswing.

We are all drawn to different rhythms of music at different times in life. Sometimes you want something upbeat so you can shake and dance, sometimes you're needing to just chill. Recognize that music is a powerful way to enhance your experience of whatever cycle you find yourself in. Sometimes silence is the best rhythm of all.

The cycle of life – birth, death and rebirth – is another way to understand this law. It is all perfectly orderly when observed from the outside, yet can be quite disorienting when experienced from within. A practice of meditation or mindfulness helps to create ease through the cycle's ups and downs. Training the mind to go with the flow will leave you experiencing almost exclusively the ups, while gliding past the downs. By recognizing the cycle from within and knowing that it is part of life, you can experience the whole process as a beautiful part of your own growth.

Jack got the news on a Friday that his mother had passed. She had not been sick, so it was quite a shock to him, his father, and his siblings. It took a day or two of tears and family bonding before he was able to come out of his fog. Katie had gotten to know her over the years as well, and pointed out how spiritual she was – how she was very clear that death is part of life. Instead of being angry, he was able to celebrate her life and trust that all would be well for her, him, and his whole family. He could feel that, even in his unknowingness, life is good.

The law of rhythm helped Jack to understand the circle of life, and celebrate life, rather than feel decimated by tragedy.

Chapter 17

LAW OF GENDER

The law of gender manifests in all things as masculine and feminine. It is this law that governs what we know as creation. The law of gender manifests in the animal kingdom as sex. This law decrees everything in nature is both male and female. Both are required for life to exist.

Everything has within it both masculine and feminine, male and female. Life cannot exist without both, and every reproductive process contains both to varying degrees. In animals, sex is the manifestation of the law of gender. People fall on a continuum with emotional and physical characteristics of feminine and masculine ranging from one extreme to the other, and every variant in between.

Another name for this law is the Law of Gestation, which governs the process by which all things grow and evolve. Every seed has within it the programming of the mature plant and the ability to create more of itself through succeeding generations. Every seed has a particular period of gestation during which it grows to maturity. Carrots, tomatoes, and oak trees all have their own time frame to become what their seeds always knew they would become. Likewise, all animals and humans have set governance for their own re-creation – for humans gestation is 280 days.

When tomato seeds are sown in different conditions, the outcome of their gestation is different as well. In rocky soil, they may germinate and begin to grow, but will not make it for lack of nutrients. Some will have their fate sealed by bugs, birds, or other animals nibbling them up for sustenance. And those that are planted in high quality, richly amended soil will be the best producers. Nurturing the plants with sun, water, and more fuel will produce unbelievable bounty.

The law of gestation also applies to the thoughts we think. Each thought, when initiated, has within it the full expression of its potential. Each thought is a seed that, when planted in fertile soil and nurtured, MUST grow to maturity. You can know, with certainty, that every thought you think wants to be fully realized. It is a very good thing that gestation kicks in and you can replace negative thoughts with positive ones before they come into being. It can take time to manifest thoughts into things, depending on their complexity and your alignment with their vibration. Every thought has within it the perfect timing for its manifestation. Keep up the nurturing by taking action and use your faith, trusting that it will be fulfilled.

Katie had an idea for a business where she would be putting together customized spa/wellness treatment packages for people based on their location – like Uber meets Ten Thousand Waves. It started with just the idea, which she wrote down in detail and kept at the forefront of her mind. She saw herself using the app that would be c reated complete with the connections for practitioners that participate in the service. She did not know how she would do it or where to begin, and she had no idea how many people would actually use it. She did, however, take steps toward the goal whenever she could and within about 6 months, had thousands of users and income flowing into the business from every direction. An idea turned into profit – the guaranteed way.

The seed of Katie's idea was planted and it bore fruit in perfect time.

Part III

GOING WITH THE FLOW: ARCHITECTURE IN ACTION

"Whatever you think the world is withholding from you, you are withholding from the world [and] you already have, but unless you allow it to flow out, you won't even know that you have it."

~ Eckhart Tolle

Your miraculous mind is capable of dreaming up anything, and you are a gift to the world like no other. You alone have what it takes to be what you were always meant to be – your best self.

This section offers you the means to really get in the groove of life, to create yourself anew and live life on purpose. You will discover your ability to re-think and re-create your results. What you believe will take center stage along with your free-will manifestation powers. Once again, you'll discover tools you can use to turn your dreams into your daily life, and just how easy it can be to live a life of abundance, harmony, and joy.

Chapter 18

OUTSIDE INSIDE OUT

> "We have no longer an outside and an inside as two separate things. Now the outside may come inside and the inside may and does go outside. They are of each other. Form and function thus become one in design and execution if the nature of materials and method and purpose are all in unison."
>
> ~ Frank Lloyd Wright

Your journey of self-discovery continues. The third part of this book discusses what you are actually learning and how to put it into action. You can now look at yourself with a different set of eyes, seeing yourself progress from identifying who you really are and how you are part of an orderly system of creation. With an increasing understanding of the laws outlined in the previous section, your toolbox for transformation is exponentially multiplied. Taking that deep understanding from theoretical to practical is what will have you creating lasting change on the inside, and improved results on the outside.

When working within a limited space, there are tricks that you can use to place windows or things beyond your windows (like plants or a garden) in a precise location to draw your view to the outside. The effect of this is to stretch the inside space and make it feel larger by visually including the space that is beyond its walls. This is referred to as bringing the outside in.

The way most people have been operating throughout their lives is observing the outside world, taking it in through their senses, and then reacting to it in order to produce more results out there in the world. Now we're swinging the doors wide open and letting the light in.

In this way, when you observe the outside world (your results), rather than just internalizing them as they are, you can always be on the lookout for more light, for a better way. From that viewpoint of looking for a better way, seeing past the typical outside barrier, and taking in the best view of what you want to see in your world and moving toward it, you engage the power within you to create worlds. When you internalize the new idea or view, and align yourself with what it feels like to experience it, you are actively turning your inside self out. Because what you are feeling on the inside is what is expressed on the outside, you are always participating in these actions. The decision is yours though, whether you are letting it happen by default or doing it actively to create the results you most desire. It boils down to a few simple steps:

- Observe your outcome objectively
- Think of another, better way
- Feel yourself experiencing it the new way
- Act on that feeling toward your better way
- Observe your outcome objectively – and repeat this creative response cycle

Your thoughts literally become things. What you think about and internalize, you bring about in your life. This is operating all the time, everywhere, and is the basis for creating changes in your life. Any type of change that you want to see in action begins with the thought about it, even if you are unaware of it. The thoughts you are thinking guide your perceptions, which directly affect your decisions and also your actions. Whatever you have been thinking in the past, and even your thoughts in the present, are really not important. No one can force you to think anything you do not want to think. Recognize that you have the power to change your thoughts about any situation in order to change your life. Surround yourself with people and ideas that are aligned with the new thoughts that you want to think. This book is an example: Read it over and over, listen to the audio version of it, do the exercises it recommends, and consider one of the other programs offered at jaybillig.com to support your thoughts with energy to grow.

Now keep in mind that fleeting thoughts get somewhat of a pass here. Picture all the little things that pass through your mind on a daily basis, like the endless stream of news or yet another silly cat video. There is so much information coming into your conscious mind all the time, and you are constantly filtering for what you want to take in. Every thought is loaded with pure possibility and has the potential to take you through to its manifestation. Your thought energy is also connected to your vibrational energy, so in order for something to manifest, it requires your being in tune with its vibration. Your awareness of this process is the beginning of having exactly what you want in life to show up, but also know that awareness must be backed up by alignment and action – action toward your ideal vision or goal.

You might be thinking, "Oh man, I'm screwed! I think negative thoughts all the time." Well, you don't have to be positive every moment of every day. The more you practice noticing your thoughts – and more importantly, how you are feeling about the situation – the more you will be able to shift from something negative to something positive. Ask yourself if what you are feeling is serving you or how you are showing up with the people around you.

When you are feeling really good, you know you are in total alignment. Notice it, encourage it, and experience what is drawn to you. On the other hand, when something feels a bit off, trust your instincts and look for what small thing you can change to have it feel better. Suppose you have an uncomfortable situation with some people you work with. They tell jokes that belittle another co-worker and have been indirectly inviting you to participate. Instead of shaming them, you find a way to compliment them and your other co-worker at the same time, being the voice of camaraderie and cooperation. You can't change anybody else, but you are in charge of you, and even small changes can have a big impact.

It is very easy to see all the things you don't want when life is being life for you, when you face challenges in your everyday existence. It is all part of the adventure to experience fear, setbacks, and disappointments, and it is also your option to look for the good in every situation. You can find the silver lining, the bright side and the spark of beauty in even the dreariest, darkest, and least appealing places. Home in on what you do want rather than what you don't want. Rather than focusing your thoughts on being sick or that you expect to be sick because you have been in the past, focus on thoughts that you are the epitome of healthy – that you are vibrant and full of well-being.

As you begin to put what you are taking in here into practice, notice the rhythm that is at work: Visualize, Intellectualize, Internalize, Actualize, Manifest. Rinse and repeat.

In other words, see it, think about it, feel it, act on it, receive the results. Based on any results that you are observing, visualize what about it could be better. Even if you have outstanding results, there is always a better way. Now take that vision and think about it, make it real for you by imagining it and then internalizing it. When you internalize the idea – your vision – you get in touch with how it feels to have it. Feeling it drives you to take action – to actualize it – and your feeling-imbued action causes a reaction, also known as manifestation or results. You have just turned the outside inside out, and you can do it with ANY area of your life.

Now you're really getting into the rhythm of positive change, playing the game of life on purpose. With both the Universe and yourself going to bat for you, you're going to be amazed at what you are capable of creating.

Chapter 19
BELIEVING IS SEEING

"Remember that both behavior and feeling spring from belief."
~ Maxwell Maltz, MD, FICS

The first action step toward achieving any goal is observing your results and changing your thoughts about them as you move in the direction of what it is you most desire. Believing – the deep knowing that a thing is yours to be or to have – is imbued in the laws of life and in any results that are showing up in your life.

Belief is a critical piece of the whole process of living out the life of your dreams. In order for belief to have the effect you want, it must be integrated into practice. You must understand that nothing comes to pass without an alignment of the thing you want with your beliefs and it is your practice of your beliefs that dictate your results. With this understanding and practice, you can achieve literally anything you desire.

There are some people who have well-founded beliefs but have not managed to meld their behavior with them, thereby producing results that they don't really want. Others might have beliefs that are completely in sync with their actions, but because they hold onto false beliefs, they end up producing results that are awful even on a good day.

Take a look inside and check to see if what you believe is backed up by good reasoning. Observe each belief independently and run it through the good reason test by writing it down. Make a list and analyze each one deeply. Why do you believe it? Where did the belief come from? Did you pick it up from a particular person or situation? You will find that some of your beliefs were planted in your subconscious mind by someone else long ago and are built on nothing but a pile of sand. As you fearlessly dig deeper, you will clearly see that some of your beliefs are downright comical.

What we believe is a product of our assessment of a given situation. Every situation is an opportunity to reassess our beliefs, ask ourselves what they are based on, and if they are serving us. As you do this, your vision of what is possible opens wide and the view of your own skills and abilities opens even wider. Your beliefs, integrated with practice and action, are like a space ship that has been freed from the clutches of gravity, flying through space with practically no effort at all. As you continually take stock of your beliefs and reassess them, your mind will be free to effortlessly take you beyond your self-imposed tethering as well.

For all time before and until May 6, 1954, it was believed that it was impossible to run a mile in less than 4 minutes. The record up until that day had stood for nearly 10 years. However, on that day, Roger Bannister broke the 4-minute barrier, and within a couple of years many others had followed suit. They believed it was possible and did it.

As with changing paradigms and your self-image, repetition and a big impact are the ways to meld your beliefs and behaviors. In other words, you've got to practice. Remember that what is embedded in the subconscious mind automatically expresses itself with and through the body. In order to change any fixed way of being (those things that are not serving your growth trajectory), new beliefs can be used to supplant the old, ineffective ones.

The limiting factor in any endeavor in life is whether or not you believe you can do it or go there. Melding belief into actions, that is, practice, is essential to effective growth. The results you get will have a direct relationship to the level of integration your beliefs and actions enjoy. You don't even need to identify the limiting beliefs, but rather focus on ones that serve you. Here is a very helpful technique to do just that:

1. Make a list of the various areas of your existence, leaving 3-4 lines of space between each area: Life itself, yourself, your body, money, love, other people, success, health/wellness, etc.

2. Under each area, write what positive, empowering beliefs you would like to have, even if it is not currently what you believe it to be. This is where you think about it.

3. Below your desired beliefs, write positive statements as if you already believed it using the verb "to be". For example, "My life is…" "I am…" "Money is…" etc.

4. Repeat these beliefs and affirmations multiple times each day.

5. Finally, and by far most importantly, go live it. Act as if your beliefs and words are true every day. Live it when you're brushing your teeth, when you're choosing what to eat, when deciding who to spend time with – live it in every decision you make.

There are many beliefs that have been taken in by your conscious mind through education, logic, upbringing, culture, and all manner of media inputs. Another, deep level of beliefs resides in the subconscious and it is these beliefs – part of your paradigm – that dictate your behavior and results. Being able to consciously and logically think about ideas is one thing, but in order for their truth to take hold, you must believe it in the depths of your being. If a thing is not held at that level of belief, changing the paradigm is the only option to get it there.

You've probably been told your whole life that "seeing is believing". Well, that gives you a very limited view of life and living from the outside in. It is easy to believe in what you can already see because it is there in front of you, like the balance of your bank account. Allowing your outside view to dictate your inside belief is, unfortunately, how most people go through life. It is the ever-present paradigm again, sneaking up on you. It gets you locked into a pattern where the results you get are based on the results you have gotten before. It is like you are in a permanent holding pattern with a dense fog all around, able to see barely as far as your arm will reach.

The immense power of Infinite Intelligence is unleashed when you understand that in fact, believing is seeing. Your view is magnified to take in infinite possibilities. Any image you hold in your conscious mind that is impressed upon the subconscious and backed up by burning desire and unwavering belief, must be expressed by the body into physical form. Believing and acting as if the object of your desire is already in your present experience moves it into form before your very eyes. Moving forward with your beliefs fully integrated with your behavior is the surest way to see whatever you have been dreaming about show up in your outward experience.

You really are capable of doing and being anything. Yes, you! Yes, anything!! It is your belief that allows it – without belief, you might as well hang up your hat. The process is totally by law: Your thinking, impressed upon the subconscious, causes your vibration, which automatically turns into actions, setting up reactions from Source Energy, which become your results. Believe it and become it.

For example, let's say you're buying your first home. At first it could seem like a daunting and unrealistic idea, like it is meant for other people and not you. However, you keep thinking about it and you warm up to the idea. You try on what it would feel like to own your very own home. You imagine yourself in it, and you picture all the things you and your family and friends will do there together.

As you practice more, the idea that seemed silly is now feeling very real. You are taking steps toward closing on the purchase because you have shifted your belief so that it is actually a possibility. Your belief in what is possible dictates your actions, and when you actually do finally sign on the dotted line and purchase the home, it is because you first believed it, not the other way around.

When you look objectively at each area of your life – work, relationships, community, etc – you will begin to understand that the outcome you are getting, the level of your results, is a direct expression of what is held in your subconscious. Your paradigm is at the heart of it, controlling literally every outcome you observe, and is made up of beliefs brought to you courtesy of generations of your ancestors and the many influences you have had up until now.

The wonderful truth is that you don't have to settle for last year's results all over again. You have to continually ask yourself what you believe is possible for you. Ask yourself what you really desire, what you believe that is holding you back, and also what your beliefs are that support you in having it. You are a creative powerhouse, endowed with everything you need to get increasingly extraordinary results time after time. By asking the question, the answer is there. You are capable of being whatever you believe you are capable of being. So understand first what you consciously believe is possible and then call it forth from All That Is by impressing your subconscious mind with that belief.

As you create the image of what you really want and get your whole being involved in it, there are two questions in particular that will short-circuit your system and stop you before you even start. If you spend any time wondering whether a big idea is going to happen or how it will happen, you're going to be waiting a very long time and it will probably never come to be. You've got to have an image of exactly what you want, and believe it is inevitable and that all the resources to fulfill its creation will be there exactly as you are ready to receive them.

Use this easy process to boost your belief in anything:

1. With a clear image in your mind, with all manner of incredible details, make a picture of what it is you want.
2. Write it down, including all the glorious details.
3. Make it real. Imagine yourself as the person who is experiencing it. Act as if it is present.
4. Live it in your conscious mind, then in your subconscious mind. Feel it NOW.

The more you repeat this process of imagining, writing, acting out, and truly feeling what it feels like to be the image you have of your dream self, the faster it will become a permanent part of your paradigm, and the faster it will be expressed through you into form. This process is by law. Test it with small things if you need to at first, so that you can believe it and see how it works. Small things are the same as big things – thoughts that have become things.

Chapter 20
CHOOSING WELL-BEING

"Every failure comes with it the seed of an equivalent advantage."
~ Napoleon Hill

As you understand more about yourself and your power to recreate your results by consistently finding better ways to do things, your beliefs about yourself and the world will shift too, and you will see that you get to choose how it will go for you.

Earlier you read about paradigms and their power over your every move. They are covered again here because they really are that powerful, and it is very easy for them to control your life if you do not increase your knowledge of them and purposely take them on.

When you come up against any obstacle, it can be broken down to a very basic choice: fear or knowing. Some other ways to refer to knowing are understanding, truth, and love. In his book, Conversations With God, Neale Donald Walsch clarifies this polarity when he says, "It is prime force. It is the raw energy that drives the engine of human experience... Fear is the energy which contracts, closes down, draws in, runs, hides, hoards, harms. [Knowing] is the energy which expands, opens up, sends out, stays, reveals, shares, heals." However you call it, it is all about your choice. You have the power to change your mind and choose something that feels better, more in harmony with what you want. With free will, you truly have the power because free will takes precedence over everything. No other person or outside condition can tell you what to think – only you can. You have the choice then, moment by moment, to choose fear or to choose knowing. Recognize too, that your choice not to choose is your choice to stay with whatever your current vibration happens to be.

Many great leaders throughout history have taught us that you become what you think about. Consider the following statement from Henry Ford: "Whether you think you can or you think you can't—you're right." And the Buddha proclaimed, "The mind is everything. What you think, you become." Likewise, "You become what you think about all day long," is traceable to Ralph Waldo Emerson and Earl Nightingale. And Wayne Dyer stated simply, "As you think, so shall you be." To add more clarity to this, you become what you think about most often, and what you allow by your vibration of belief and knowing. It's a good thing that we don't become everything we think about, or it would be a pretty crazy mixed up world. The key to understand here is that it is what we focus on and are in harmony with that really matters.

Thoughts, or ideas when a group of thoughts are combined, are energy just like everything in the physical world is energy, except that thoughts are the most powerful form of creative energy we know of. There is a constant stream of energy flowing into and through everything, including people. When we think, we tap into that energy and form thoughts directly from it.

When we emotionalize – internalize – our thoughts, we change the vibration of the subconscious mind and we change the vibration of our body, which is a vehicle of the mind. <u>Feeling</u> is what we call our awareness of our vibration. If you are feeling great about something, you say, "I feel good," not "I am consciously aware of my positive vibration." Likewise, if you feel bad, it is because of your own negative vibration, the thought you have emotionalized.

This happens whether or not you are actually aware it is going on.

Whatever ideas are put through to the subconscious mind with repetition become embedded there, and are known as habits. A group of habits is known as a paradigm, and almost all of our paradigms are passed down genetically. The vibration you are in – the way you feel – is caused by the paradigm and it does not care whether the feeling is good or bad. The paradigm directs our feelings and we get very familiar and comfortable with those feelings, most often preferring comfort over change.

It is easy to see why people get the same results time after time when you understand that paradigms are causing their actions, and their actions are causing their results. Consistency is the order of the day with these things, fighting every step of the way to maintain the status quo in everybody.

The metaphor that says, "the apple does not fall far from the tree" is another way of recognizing that paradigms can easily cross generational lines as well. Mostly genetic, but also the results of conditioning by childhood caregivers of every kind, well meaning adults pass down all of their own programming to the children they look after. This is evident with patterns of economics, education, discipline, social standing, and pretty much every way that people operate habitually. You don't have to look very far to see examples of this in families where poverty and welfare span over generations, as if it is the norm. Yet in other families, the programming is for financial independence at the earliest possible age. You can see how the effects of even one paradigm can have a life-long impact on a person.

With paradigms being so strong, in order to get different results, it is the paradigm that must be changed. And changing them requires thinking in ways that most people have never thought before. The element you have control over is the thoughts you think, and creating different results means consciously choosing what you are thinking. It requires establishing new habit patterns in your thinking, and in many cases beginning to truly think for the first time. Every thought you think is a choice to either be in fear, which leads to energetic dis-ease and disintegration, or to be in knowing, which leads to well-being and growth.

As patterns of thought change, it changes the vibration a person is in, and when vibration changes, feelings will change too – remember, feeling is the word we use to describe our vibration. Now for small changes, this is usually not a big deal. It is when you start to entertain big, life-changing ideas that you run into trouble with your whole system. You have introduced a vibration that is totally incompatible with your current one and this is where your operating system says, "hey, wait a minute!"

Recognize that voice as your paradigm – one you are very used to obeying. We all obey our paradigm, which is why it is so important to be able to recognize it for what it is and, if it is not serving us, change it to something that does. The choice is yours to align with fear or to align with knowing. Without a doubt, knowing is your best option every time.

Chapter 21

GROWING THROUGH FEAR

"People have a hard time letting go of their suffering. Out of a fear of the unknown, they prefer suffering that is familiar."

~ Thich Nhat Hanh

Aligning yourself with knowing does not mean you will not be faced with fear time and time again, but it certainly sets you up for growth.

Every one of us has come up against fear blocking our road toward growth. Unfortunately, for nearly everybody, there is not an understanding of how the system works at all or why such fear persists. They return to business as usual, to the safety of what they know, comforting themselves with a big fat lie that has been told since the stone age: It is better to be safe than sorry. There is absolutely no growth in the status quo.

To experience growth, fear is part of the package deal. When you stand up to your fears, growth is automatic. You've got a picture of what you want and your desire for that thing is what will buoy you up so you can let go of your past and tell your old paradigm to take a hike. With ongoing study and understanding you can burst right through the blockade and claim the life you were meant to live.

There was a man who was afraid of deep water. He avoided it for years, and kept his panic at bay, until a friend signed him up for a whitewater kayaking course. On the very first day of the training, the students were taught how to safely escape from an overturned boat, which involves being completely upside down under the water. He was a total bundle of nerves; convincing himself that purposely flipping his boat with him still inside was a death sentence. He put it off as long as possible and went last among the group of trainees. When he finally found himself submerged, time stood still and he was able to pause, knowing that there was nothing to fear at all. He gracefully removed himself from the boat and came to the surface of the water for air. It was the first time he had allowed himself to relax enough to realize the fear was all in his head.

There is a systematic process that you go through to get from captivity to freedom. Each step is defined below and laid out to show its impact on your life.

Captivity – Consideration – Friction – Freedom

<u>Captivity</u> is where you are, locked in with your paradigm and current results. Your view of the world from captivity is based only on what you observe about your present results, and since your paradigm agrees wholeheartedly with you, you keep getting more of the same. Your own programming is holding you hostage – you are holding yourself hostage – and you are vibrating at a very comfortable frequency. It is comfortable because it is what you know, not because it is objectively pleasant in most cases.

With <u>consideration</u>, you begin to think, to entertain new ideas, to try on a different way of being. You do it because we are all programmed with the desire for expansion. You are using your imagination and reasoning factor to look at what you want and create a mental image of it. You say you want to change, and thinking about it is both fun and feels good. Your conscious mind is thinking about choosing something outside the box, which can be both exciting and scary at the same time, but you have not gotten emotionally involved with the idea. Because of this, your vibration remains in your comfort zone and it is only your conscious mind that is testing the waters.

Next you get really involved with your new way of thinking. You totally fall in love with the idea and you can see yourself living in the new way. You believe it. Your belief puts you in a new vibration and it is totally at odds with the vibration you are so comfortable and familiar with. This creates some major <u>friction</u>. You really want to move forward and have what you've been dreaming of. The new vibration is totally foreign and will take some getting used to. All the while your paradigm is giving you every reason in the world not to rock the boat. There is literally friction between the two vibrations in your subconscious mind, and body. This is where most people come up against a giant wall of fear and bounce right off of it, back into the comfort of their mundane existence, right back to captivity where it feels familiar and "ok."

It takes courage to embrace the new vibration and make it your new paradigm. What stops people is ignorance, which can only be overcome with knowledge and awareness. Not being able to see how their dream will come true, or what resources are ready to jump to their aid on the other side of the wall of fear holds people back. Their paradigm kicks into high gear and, fueled by ignorance, their picture gets diminished. It is easy to give in to negative thoughts and ideas, which of course keep them in a negative vibration. Remember, though, that fear and growth are companions and that you must move through fear to experience real growth.

<u>Freedom</u> comes through knowledge and knowledge comes about through diligent inquiry – there is no other way. There are many different kinds of inquiry, but knowledge is not possible without it. With knowledge, you can move through the fear and into true freedom. Freedom brings with it your new vibration, which reprograms your subconscious mind with a new paradigm. This is now your new conditioning, which you can count on for some friction the next time you go after another new goal.

Does this mean that you will never experience your old way of being again? Not at all. It means that you now know what it feels like to take on your paradigms and fears, and move through them to freedom. You are experiencing the growth that goes hand in hand with fear. Your next new idea will be another opportunity for growth as well. The more you gain an understanding of how your marvelous mind works – by law, remember – you will be better equipped to recognize your paradigm for what it is. You will be able to tell it you're not afraid and before you know it, you'll be growing by leaps and bounds.

When the wall of fear stands in your way, there are some things to keep in mind that will help you move through it to freedom.

- Take a deep breath first and know that there is nothing to worry about.
- You don't have to settle for your current programming. Most people are not aware they are running on autopilot and on someone else's version of system software. You are a creative being, an incredible expression of Infinite Intelligence, and you are now choosing an upgrade – your free will upgrade – to a much better version.
- Your desire and passion for what you want, your fire for seeing your new life purpose through, will be needed to break free from captivity. If you're not in love with the idea, the fear will win – but if you are, nothing can stop you.
- Be objective about the fears and all the negativity, identifying which version of software you're running on. Understanding its source will help you to step right through it. Observe the old way and have faith; know that through the unknown lies the upgrade.
- You've been up against this wall of fear before, and most likely if you failed to move through it, you were stopped by your paradigms and some old software that is caught in an infinite repeat loop. It's like you're turning the lights on your past for the first time and it is illuminating your way forward. Facing your fear head on is the switch.

- Your paradigms want all of this to look impossible, for every small step to seem like a big hurdle. Its job is to keep the current system in place. It will try every excuse in the book to stop your growth and will hit hard with your greatest fear. It is nothing but a thick fog though, and you can march right on through. The light within you will burn it off and you will realize it is nothing but vapor.

The only mind you have to make up is your own. Your cycle of captivity, consideration, friction, and freedom is ongoing as you take on new ideas and new ways of being. You can languish in captivity, in comfort, or you can go for growth. Fear has nothing on knowing – choose knowing, and freedom!

Chapter 22

GIVING IS RECEIVING

"Harvest the good. Forgive all the rest."
~ Michael Bernard Beckwith

By now you are seeing that beyond just understanding yourself and the laws of life, how you show up in the world really matters. Your choice for well-being goes hand in hand with your resolve to take on fear and grow. All of the tools you've been learning and applying are phenomenal to use on your transformation, and even more powerful when you give of yourself to the rest of the world.

Leave everyone with the impression of increase. Wherever you go, in every way, with every person, make them feel better for having had an interaction with you. You are the embodiment of the Life Force and you cannot run out of it. When you give it away, you create more – also known as circulation. It is according to the law of cause and effect that this happens. The act of giving something away is proof that you have it to give and by law, it must come back to you.

You and everyone you come in contact with are spiritual beings having a human experience. You are connected and are literally of one Source, expressed in one and infinite ways. The one way is pure Source Energy and the infinite ways are pure Source Energy. Inherent in all life – that is, every expression of Source Energy, seen and unseen – is the desire to grow and expand in as big a way as possible.

Look around and observe the physical world. In any plant, its ability to reproduce is not limited to one replication. It is programmed to create sometimes millions of seeds from the one that was initially germinated. Those same seeds are consumed as food for many creatures and carried off by the wind to be planted and turned into countless offspring generation after generation. Talk about expansion! Across the realm of fauna the same evidence can be seen, producing multiple copies of the next best version of themselves over and over. Human beings, with mostly one birth at a time, are naturally set up for many offspring. Even the planet is continually turning itself inside out and expanding its rock foundation to support more plants, animals, and people.

Our natural inclination in living is to want to experience a more expansive version of it. Athletes want a better score the next time, or to set a new personal record for themselves, for their team, or the world. Students want to do better on their next report card and get into their top choice of university or grad school. Investors want to expand their portfolios and businesses are forever seeking to increase their profits.

As physical expressions of Source Energy, growth cannot be curtailed. Source is always for more. And so, when you give more, by law, you gain more. If you seek to gain without giving, thinking there is not enough to go around and you must get your share, you are coming from a place of lack and so you will experience lack.

When you give and leave everybody with the feeling of expansion, you are tapping into Source for yourself, and into their connection to Source as well. You are in harmony with their natural inclination to expand and it feels good for all of you. When you feel good in giving this way, you will be inviting good things and feelings right back to you. You are setting up a magnetic force, drawing good things into your life.

As you do this with everyone, you will be in an incredible vibration and your giving nature and abundance will be apparent. Your spontaneous actions always show the world the truth about what you believe and what habits you have internalized. Turn this practice into a habit and everybody you touch will be better off for it. Your realm will be filled with your own expansion, and people and things around you will be expanding too. Give freely and willingly.

Keep it up and you will soon reprogram your paradigm with this way of approaching the world. When you do, you will also need to be ready and willing to receive all the good that will be headed your way. It is by repetition that your paradigm gets reset, so the more you give, the more you will receive. Receive whatever comes to you with joy, humility, and grace. Know that it is by law that what you have put out is coming back to you – there is no other way for it to come to you. By giving and receiving from the same positive vibration, you are the source of your own abundance. You are circulating the Life Force, or as Wallace D. Wattles refers to it in his transformative book, *The Science of Getting Rich*, originally published in 1910, the "Thinking Stuff." In the summary, he emphasizes to give to everyone "a use value in excess of the cash value [you] receive, so that each transaction makes for more life… and that the impression of increase will be communicated to all with whom [you] come in contact." By acting in this way, he states that what you "receive will be in exact proportion to the definiteness of [your] vision, the fixity of [your] purpose, the steadiness of [your] faith, and the depth of [your] gratitude."

Our paradigm, remember, is what controls our every move. So if you find yourself reacting to a situation with a negative feeling, you will find the source somewhere deep inside. The negative situation you find yourself in is happening when you are on autopilot, or you would not be choosing it. You don't really even need to dig for it, but rather look for a different way of doing things; a way where everybody wins and you are giving your most expansive self to everybody you meet.

This is part of a life-long practice. Your paradigm will creep onto the scene at some very inopportune times, but it does not know it is that way for you. It is just doing its job of keeping your life in the realm of the known. It is up to you to put in some different programming – such as the impression of increase for all you touch – and get that to be your new operating system. There is always a newer, better version of software out there. By practicing more unconditional giving, you essentially sign up for the auto-update plan. You align yourself with the flow of all abundance when, for example, you automatically reach into your pocket when someone asks for money on the street corner, or when you point out what you really like about your colleague.

There are people right now that we all have in our lives who would benefit from being left with the feeling of expansion. A clerk at the store or a coworker, a neighbor or a stranger, every one of them is an opportunity for you to be more so they can be more. When you give expansively, you are raising your own vibration and the vibration of whomever is the recipient of your giving. Look for the best in people and point it out to them. It might be someone who really bugs you or that you have a long history of animosity with. This can be really hard at first as we overcome past ways of thinking and being. Start with one tiny thing if you need to, like a sincere compliment, or simply being thankful for how their presence helps you grow.

Rest assured, when you do put this into practice and it becomes a habit, you will be the recipient of so much good flowing into your life it will be hard to keep up – the law of cause and effect makes it so. It is most likely the case that what comes back to you will not be coming from the same person or place you gave it to. Don't worry for a second about that. Know that you and your giving are tapped into All That Is, and that it is from the One Source that you are receiving as well. It is not possible to give too much. Expect goodness to flow to you and through you. Open yourself up and be a conduit for goodness by giving opulently and receiving abundantly.

One of the best practices to have you increasing the circulation of abundance and well-being in your life is to be grateful. You can practice it every day with everything around you. Keep a gratitude journal or notebook where you write down what you are grateful for and what you appreciate as you encounter it. Visit jaybillig.com and download a free gratitude pad you can use to help you get in the habit of daily thanks. The action of being grateful cannot happen if you are not in a good vibration, so when you look around you and notice what you are thankful for, it necessarily creates more positive vibration. Also, giving thanks is a sure way to prove anything is present and accounted for in your life. As you practice gratitude, and thus giving is receiving, try these steps:

1. Write down 10 things you are grateful for. They can be things already in your life or things you are thankful for in advance of having, doing, or being them.
2. Relax and breathe deeply for about 5 minutes.
3. Send good thoughts and energy to some people who bother you.

You have infinite potential locked up inside you. Even if you have achieved some really great things, your potential to grow is exponential: Understanding yourself and your connection to universal laws is your key to unleashing it. With understanding comes freedom – the freedom to choose anything you desire and the freedom to think far beyond what you ever thought possible for yourself.

You can create your own paradigm, continually replacing old ones with new ones that serve you better. You can reject anything that is not serving you and look for a better way, diving into the deep where others would never even consider going. Expand your thinking and you expand your world.

Deeply connecting with other people who support your big dreams for yourself is also an important piece of the giving/receiving process. You have immeasurable gifts and you have a lot to share. You also cannot do it all with regards to achieving every goal you have set out to achieve. There are others willing and able to receive what you have to give and give what you need.

In every way, give your best, be your best self, and in every moment the next best version of yourself. You will attract people, circumstances, and things to help you along the way. Use the obstacles you encounter to learn and grow, and let them pump you up. You get to decide what you become and it is amazing! The world is waiting for YOU!

Chapter 23

EVERYDAY EASE

"Imperfect action is better than no action at all."
~ Peggy McColl and Brian Proctor

Giving your best self, as we explored in the last chapter, will help you to experience life on purpose. When you are receiving abundantly, you will be able to observe the power that is in you to create your world. From the space of generosity and graciousness, we will now explore some very effective actions that can help your level of results skyrocket.

Habits are the little things in life that we do automatically that either keep us moving forward or hold us back. Being able to establish new habits and stick to them is critical to having a life of ease.

Every habit begins as an idea. People who are living life very effectively know how to use their creative power to come up with ideas that they can turn into habits to help them move toward any objective. They are able to identify things that are not working in their life and turn them into things that are.

Identifying one's own productive habits and buoying them with practice is certainly important, but equally important is being able to listen to and learn from others. Picking up habits from others is very natural because we learned to do it as young children and have been doing it our whole lives. Habits that don't serve us are a dime a dozen so it is critical to be able to reject them and instead seek to emulate people who have highly effective habits.

As an example, look at the many people who have integrated meditation or mindfulness practice into their daily lives. Oprah Winfrey stated that, after a meditation, she felt "full of hope, a sense of contentment, and deep joy. Knowing for sure that even in the daily craziness that bombards us from every direction, there is – still – the constancy of stillness. Only from that space can you create your best work and your best life."

Bob Proctor speaks about his habit of getting out of bed very early every day, going to his office by 5:30 AM, and using the early morning time to do his best studying and productive work for the day ahead. He is among the most successful people out there in the world of personal development having built multiple companies operating all across the globe.

In 1984, determined to get to the Virgin Islands on time, being told at the airport that his final flight (and the last flight of the night) had been cancelled, Richard Branson took action. He went and chartered a private airplane to take him to the Virgin Islands, which he said he did not have the money to do. Then, he picked up a small blackboard, wrote "Virgin Airlines. $39." on it, and went over to the group of people who had been on the flight that was cancelled. He sold tickets for the rest of the seats on the plane, used their money to pay for the chartered plane, and they all went to the Virgin Islands that night. You probably know the rest of the story. This just shows that successful people start before they feel ready.

Do not be afraid when someone else comes up with an idea that is a better way of doing something. In fact, embrace it and, giving full credit to the person who thought of it, take it on as your own. Always be open to seeing a better, more effective way and incorporating it into your routine.

Understand that you are a creative powerhouse and it is up to you to take command of your own life. Be very clear of the direction you are going and use your habits for your own benefit and the benefit of those around you. There is no need to compete, only create. Your creative essence, aligned with the creative essence of others will have all of you tapping into the infinite source of supply.

Having a GPS system or map on a mobile device is an incredible piece of technology. With it, we are able to put in our destination – our goal – and be directed to the shortest, most efficient path to take. When you plug in the place you want to go, the system basically goes into a holding pattern. As long as you sit there, the map will be laid out for you, but the interactive guidance will be on pause. The moment you begin to move, however, all the forces of the system are called up and you are guided along the route.

The goal of the system is your goal and it must get you there no matter what. It pays attention to unseen conditions beyond your reach and helps you avoid potential roadblocks. If you take a turn or a side trip for food or fuel, it automatically recalculates a new route based on where you are to get you where you want to go.

Whenever you have a clearly defined goal and are passionate about its attainment, the Energy of the Universe works as your GPS. You can talk about a goal all day long, write about it, envision it and proclaim it to the world, but unless you put yourself in gear and take action in its direction, the system will remain paused. Once you take a step, all the forces of the unseen are marshaled for you and it knows the most efficient route to take. As long as you keep taking steps toward your goal, the system will recalibrate and keep you on track, even if you get off course. With your goal – and your burning desire to fulfill it – Source Energy is put in motion to achieve it. You truly cannot fail unless you quit.

Keep focused on where you are going and know that you do not need to know how. You have a plan – a map – of one possible way. Follow your plan and be open and nimble so that as you discover better and better ways of reaching your goal, you can adjust the waypoints as you go. Remain focused on the end and you will get there. Let's look at some steps to help you along the way:

- Set a very clear, detailed goal.
- Brainstorm some possible ways to get there by yourself, and also include other people who support you fulfilling your dreams – ALL options are on the table.
- Pick one way and write out a plan for it, even if it seems unrealistic and exceedingly unlikely.
- Take a step forward following your plan.
- As you inevitably have missteps along the way, continually ask these questions:

"What am I doing?" "What's working?" "What's not working?"

- Adjust to what is working and bolster it with more of the same.
- Objectively look at what is not working, find the opposite, and try that instead.
- Continually refocus on your goal and keep moving!

Albert E.N. Gray discovered and shared with the world the common denominator of success that every successful person has "formed the habit of doing things that failures don't like to do." He went on to say that,

> "*Successful people are influenced by the desire for pleasing results. Failures are influenced by the desire for pleasing methods and are inclined to be satisfied with such results as can be obtained by doing things they like to do.*"
>
> "*Every single qualification for success is acquired through habit. People form habits and habits form futures. If you do not deliberately form good habits, then unconsciously you will form bad ones. You are the kind of person you are because you have formed the habit of being that kind of person, and the only way you can change is through changing habits.*"

When you decide to make a promise to yourself to make some new habits, you're going to have to also make the habit of making new habits. In other words, it is important to continually be on the lookout for what you are doing, what is working, and what is not working so that you can adjust your actions accordingly. If you're not used to making new habits or it does not come to you easily, this too can be learned. Making habits and sticking to them is the name of the game here. What makes them sticky? Well, there really is only one thing and that is having a clearly defined goal that you're passionate about. Keeping a new habit has to have a purpose behind it, and you've got to be inspired by it or you might as well just stop now.

Let's look at making new habits, made simple. Take out a piece of paper and write down your own answers to the following:

1. What habits do you notice that you do the same way everyday? Example: drink a cup of coffee in the morning, brush your teeth before going to bed, sleep on the left side of the bed, read something, etc.

2. What new habits have you tried to implement that have not been successful? Example: exercise daily, calling your mother or father once a week, arriving on time to work everyday, etc.

3. What habits would you like to have on a daily basis that would serve you and your ideal vision or goals? Look to your heart, deep inside, to find these answers.

4. Recognize that your paradigm, being a group of habits, is at work in all of these questions. In order to make habits permanent, it takes practice, persistence, and a focus on your burning desire until such time as your new habit or habits are integrated into your paradigm, your operating system.

5. You can further ease the integration of new habits by breaking down what you wrote on your piece of paper for number 3 above to mini habits that all are part of the larger one and

then, backed up by your passion, implement them one or two at a time.

When a new habit is no longer new and its everyday practice is automatic, then you'll see your whole world change. You'll see that you can do ANYTHING you make a decision to do and stick to. You'll see that you probably aimed too low and that your ability to put any new habit into practice is easier with each try. You're getting really good at it and it really is easy!

Chapter 24

MAKING MUSIC WITH LIFE

"Practice does not make perfect – it makes permanent."
~ Alexander Libermann

Every word of this book has been about you: Your inherent awesomeness, infinite potential, and stunning beauty; your creative power in a perfectly ordered universe; and your ability to choose that which you desire and claim it as your own.

Habits are the little things in life that we do automatically that either keep us moving forward or hold us back. Being able to establish new habits and stick to them is critical to having a life of ease.

Chances are, even if you had a very clear picture of what you want to create out of life, having the question posed again in this context brought new ideas and images to the forefront. In answering the question, "What do you want?" you call forth from the ether your very own, completely customized and personalized design for the perfect manifestation of your idea.

Expanding on that initial question and really digging into not just what you want, but rather what inspires you at the core of your being is completely exhilarating and simultaneously, a pretty scary proposition. An ideal vision of your life purpose and goals is enough to create a burning desire so hot that nothing can stop you.

Well, nothing but yourself and your paradigms can stop you. Your paradigms are also what guide you when you're totally on track, so they play a very important role in your life. All of your paradigms are dedicated to keeping your operating system going. By recognizing the difference between ones that serve you and ones that are less than ideal for your growth and then committing to replace the non-productive ones with very valuable and productive ones, you are setting yourself up for being able to keep your fire of desire burning bright – and seeing your dreams come true.

Thinking in pictures comes naturally to everybody and the thing nobody has ever seen is the mind. With a picture, however, you begin to uncover how the mind really works, and get it. The mind can be easily understood as having two parts – the conscious mind and subconscious mind – and the stickperson image further reveals that the body is a vehicle of the mind. The conscious mind is where you think and where your senses are connected, while the subconscious mind is where you feel (or vibrate). Whatever vibration you are in determines what happens with the body. So seeing your mind gives you the ability to see everything in your world as you have never seen it before.

Along with your five senses that are perfect for taking in the outside world, you are gifted with six higher mental faculties that, when understood and applied, can have you operating at warp speed. The imagination is the most powerful force in the world, creating literally everything that now exists. Intuition is your direct connection to Infinite Intelligence and when tuned in, never fails you. Will is your attraction super power since what you focus on you draw to yourself. Your memory can be trained to remember on purpose by using ridiculous association. With reason, you think and can thus continually improve on your results by thinking of new ways to do anything. And finally, perception allows you to change your view of anything and thus to change the very thing you are looking at. Wrap them all together and strengthen them with practice, and watch your intellectual prowess grow far beyond what you have ever known yourself to have before.

You have a front row seat to your self-image on display, controlling how you show up in the world. Having the knowledge that it is your own personal rendering that determines your results, you can change your self-image and write the script of the life you most desire. Are you ready for your spotlight?

Learning that there are rules to how life works and that everybody gets the same deal in life completely levels the playing field. You met Jack and Katie and got to experience the laws of life along with them—you are on this parallel journey. You recognize that there is only One, that All That Is is all you, and that everything, including your thoughts, is in a constant state of vibration, at different frequencies. Action is necessary for anything to come to be and there is a corresponding existence in both physical and spiritual realms. Circulation has every effect perfectly associated to a traceable cause and every abundance flows from an infinite source of supply. Your vibration sets up an attractive force, magnetizing whatever you are feeling to you. Every thought and every thing, which is all pure energy, is in constant state of change and nothing is created or destroyed. Everything just is until it is measured relative to something else and everything, in its wholeness, contains polar opposites. There is a rhythm to life, an ebb and flow, and every seed – including thought seeds – contains the programming for its gestation and ultimate manifestation. You've learned A LOT – let's play!

As you have gained an understanding of what makes the real you tick, and also the unbreakable rules of the game, you have been given tools to transform yourself from within. Your power of objective self-reflection allows you to observe any results and recalibrate your actions, turning your outside inside out and producing very different results.

In order for those different results to take form, you have learned that you've got to believe it. You've got to believe that your dream is yours to have, and when you do, feeling what it feels like to have it and acting as if it is already your present reality will, by law, make it so. Believing, indeed, is seeing.

It's pretty amazing that your life boils down to one choice, don't you think? That's right, just like you've explored here, every moment of every day is a choice for fear or knowing. Fear leads to dis-ease and disintegration, while knowing leads to well-being and continual growth. Are you choosing well-being?

Finding yourself face to face with your fears is a natural part of the process of growth and there is, in fact, no way to grow without it. Moving from your vibration in a state of captivity to consideration on to friction and finally freedom takes burning desire backed up with faith and persistence. Growing through fear is far preferable to remaining in paradigm-imposed lockup, so choose, don't lose.

You know about the circulation in your body, and likewise it is with the flow of abundance – or plenty – in your life. The purpose of any abundance is to provide comfort and magnify whatever is held in the heart of the person who is its guardian. Together with sincere gratitude, you set yourself up for receiving graciously when you are giving willingly and thus you see, giving is receiving.

You have all sorts of habits you go through life with, and you now have the tools to add a few more that can serve you in many ways toward the realization of your goals and dreams. Habits are your daily companions anyway, so you might as well use them to create some everyday ease.

Life is so beautiful if you let it be, and get out of your own way. Allow yourself to feel the rhythm of life and know that there are not any accidents, that you are perfect in your Spiritual Essence. Failures and mistakes along the way are your self-discovery mechanism and the way you re-tune to your goals. They are there for you to learn and refocus on your objectives.

You are the conductor of your own orchestra and chorus. Well, not just the conductor, but also the strings, winds, horns, percussion, and voices. Step back and listen to the sounds you make and those you are having reflected back to you because of what you are putting out. If something is out of rhythm or out of tune, spend more time practicing the new sound you want to hear. As you put all of this into practice, it is like hearing voices in perfect harmony, feeling totally moved by the perfect alignment of the whole orchestra.

There is an old tale that goes something like this: A maestro is rushing up the street in New York City when he is stopped by a stranger who asks, "Can you tell me how to get to Carnegie Hall?" "Yes," said the breathless maestro, "Practice! Practice! Practice!"

Keep in mind that virtuosity is a lifetime pursuit. The way to be a virtuoso with your life is to practice living it to its fullest every moment of every day. Never stop dreaming. Take the time to learn something new about yourself, to explore the unknown. Make a habit of gratitude and happiness. Practice being in action, even when your action is silence and resting. Discover your best practices and be open to replacing ones that may not be serving you any longer.

Your life is the adventure of learning and joy that you make it. Every moment is an opportunity to find the joy in it and know that there is nothing wrong. Every mistake is something to welcome and even celebrate because it is a snapshot of exactly where you are at the moment, and a clear indication of what needs your attention next as you become more and more yourself through learning.

The only reason to be alive is to fully, and simply, live life. You get to choose if it will be simple and easy or complicated and difficult. Go all in with life and you will set it up so that you experience all of it in abundance, easily. For the experience of it is the best reason to do just about anything you can think of. When you are in that space, you continually bring more of yourself to the party that is life. When you show up with your gifts that you happily and willingly give, and you are also a gracious receiver, the flow of life lived fully is in sync.

Vision, beliefs, and actions are the gist of success. They are the three pillars of anything that comes to you in life, and you get to decide the level of anything you want to experience. Dream big and set your vision high. Remember, it takes the same amount of effort as aiming low. Believe it and receive it. Align your beliefs with your vision in order for it to be a vibrational match, and it will be magnetized to you. Move in the direction of your dream – keep going – and it must come to pass.

Here you have found the foundation as well as the whole process to transform any raw materials – including your life – into anything you can imagine. You are a perfect and complete, totally unique, and ever-changing manifestation of Life Itself. You get to decide – now – what your next best manifestation will be. Go!

More about Jay

Jay Billig is an author, teacher, mentor and coach who has been inspiring people to dream big and creatively transform their own lives for over 20 years. His thinking as a transformationalist has been there his whole life in one form or another: from developing a series of convertible tables out of simple concrete pavers and wood boards to transforming the least appealing buildings into masterpieces. After attending The University of St. Thomas in St. Paul, without graduating, he decided to follow his desire for service and move to Austin, Texas, where he learned from seasoned leaders – and taught himself – what he needed to be a successful entrepreneur in residential building, architectural design and real estate investment. He spent over two decades helping people transform their lives by transforming their spaces. This has evolved into his passion for helping people to see themselves as transformationalists as well. Jay's unique gift is that he seamlessly blends science, spirituality and practical tools to help individuals and organizations transform the space within themselves so that their presence in the world is transformed. Born in Little Falls, MN into an eclectic clan of thirteen siblings, Jay's personal path of transformation is ongoing and his love of learning is a constant companion. Jay, his partner, and their five children, are citizens of the earth, with a particular fondness for Austin, Texas.

Where to go from here

Now that you have discovered your Architect within, there are a lot of opportunities to continue the conversation with free resources and additional services at jaybillig.com.

Visit jaybillig.com to take advantage these free transformation resources:

- Download and print your very own goal card.
- Your personal gratitude pad for ramping up your thanks every day.
- Register for daily *Transformation Groove* emails delivered right to your inbox to keep you inspired and reminded of your awesomeness.

And don't miss out on these amazing tools:

- *Transformation Sessions* – Subscribe to weekly live calls with Jay and have all of your questions answered about your own transformation as well as *Architect of Being* and how to apply it in your life.
- *Transformation Stream* – Subscribe to monthly interviews and classes with Jay and amazing transformation experts, designed to inspire and enrich you with content that is not available anywhere else.
- *Transforming You* Program. Download a self-study course to keep your personal transformation and life on purpose.
- *Group Coaching* – Sign up to spend quality time with Jay and other transformationalists for a special 8 week program together to ramp up your effectiveness and manifestation.
- *One-on-One Mentoring* – Apply to work directly with Jay, personalized to fit your needs, with very limited slots available.

jaybillig.com

CPSIA information can be obtained
at www.ICGtesting.com
Printed in the USA
LVOW12*2150140616
492637LV00005B/5/P